THE POWER OF ACCOUNTING

The Power of Accounting: What the Numbers Mean and How to Use Them provides a highly readable text for non-financial managers. It explores accounting's uses and limitations in the management process. The text is intended for users of accounting information as opposed to preparers. It focuses on aiding the reader in understanding what accounting numbers mean, what they do not mean, when and how they can be used for decision making and planning and when they cannot.

Larry Lewis is a Professor of Accounting at the University of Portland's Pamplin School of Business, USA. He earned his B.A. and M.A. from the University of Missouri, and his Ph.D. from the University of Nebraska. He served as the Dr. Robert B. Pamplin, Jr. School of Business Dean from June of 2001 to June of 2006. He currently teaches accounting at both the graduate and undergraduate levels and is a consultant to businesses, government organizations, and non profits.

THE POWER OF ACCOUNTING

What the Numbers Mean and How to Use Them

Larry Lewis

Routledge
Taylor & Francis Group

NEW YORK AND LONDON

First published 2012
by Routledge
711 Third Avenue, New York, NY 10017

Simultaneously published in the UK
by Routledge
2 Park Square, Milton Park, Abingdon, Oxon OX14 4RN

Routledge is an imprint of the Taylor & Francis Group, an informa business

© 2012 Taylor & Francis

Library of Congress Cataloging-in-Publication Data
Lewis, Larry (Lawrence D.), 1941–
    The power of accounting : what the numbers mean and how to use them / Larry Lewis.
    p. cm.
    Includes index.
    1. Accounting. I. Title.
    HF5636.L49 2011
    657—Sdc23
                    2011033066

ISBN: 978–0–415–88430–3 (hbk)
ISBN: 978–0–415–88431–0 (pbk)
ISBN: 978–0–203–12909–8 (ebk)

Typeset in Baskerville
by Swales & Willis Ltd, Exeter, Devon
Printed and bound in the United States of America on acid-free paper
by Edwards Brothers, Inc.

To my wife, Adele, without whose support, encouragement and considerable editing skills this book would not have been possible.

CONTENTS

ACKNOWLEDGMENTS

I wish to thank publisher John Szilagyi, his very able administrative assistant Sara Werden, copy-editor Helen Moss, Tamsin Ballard at Swales and Willis and the editorial staff at Routledge for their generous help and support. I also want to thank the reviewers who took the time and effort to provide useful comments, suggestions and valuable critiques.

Special thanks go to some very capable persons who had a direct hand in editing, organizing, gathering data and providing invaluable aid in helping me navigate the electronic jungle. They are Adele Lewis, Kat Cottrell, Kacia Hicks, Joy Huff, Alex Kenefick and Sarah Klemsz.

Any mistakes in the text are solely mine. I welcome your comments and suggestions for further improvement.

We are drowning in information while starving for wisdom.
(E.O. Wilson, *Consilience*)

There will be companies that excel. And occasionally they will excel because of luck. But usually they excel because of brains.
(Warren Buffett, speaking about
Apple's Steve Jobs on Fox Business Network)

Mors ultima ratio. [Death is the final accounting.]
(Anonymous – Latin)

INTRODUCTION

This book is about understanding and using the information that accounting systems provide and which managers need in order to be successful. It is written for those who work in any type of organization, large or small, corporate or non-corporate, and want to become more effective managers.

Accounting has been called the language of business and in a very real sense it is. Studying business through the lens of accounting provides a perspective accessible through no other discipline. Accounting takes you deep inside an organization. Every transaction an organization undertakes has an impact on its financial well-being. Accounting tracks those transactions and reports their effects.

If you want to be an expert on France, you would do well to learn the French language. If you want to be an expert on Latin America, a solid knowledge of Spanish would be a great asset. If you want to understand the game of baseball, you need to understand its lingo. So it is with business and its language.

Accounting is part of the bedrock of our culture and economic system. Consider the following: Most of us were brought into this world in a very sophisticated, complex organization – a hospital. The clothes we wear, the food we eat, the cars we drive, the gasoline we put in those cars and the education we receive come to most of us through organizations. When we die it's more than likely we'll be laid to rest by an organization. In other words, virtually every aspect of our lives, in one way or another, is affected by organizations.

It's probably impossible to overstate the importance of the role organizations play in our daily lives. Take them away and we would live in a very different society. Without the information accounting provides to managers of these organizations, commerce as we know it today would not exist. Rather, it would probably be carried on through some sort of rudimentary barter-style economy.

All the organizations we depend so much on cannot stay in business without effective management. Read the business section of your local newspaper for a week and note the businesses and non-profit organizations that are quitting operations. For one reason or another, these organizations did not satisfy the needs of their potential customers in an effective manner. So, perhaps it is not hyperbole after all to say that organizations are central to our well-being and our way of life and that accounting plays a very important role by providing information necessary for their effective management.

As a manager, your performance is very likely to be evaluated on the basis of accounting numbers. (Did you meet your budget? Are your overhead costs under control? What drives those overhead costs? What are the profits and return on investment your division earned this past quarter?) Understanding what accounting numbers mean, what they don't mean and how they can be used for your benefit is vital to your success.

There are a couple of different ways to study accounting and finance. One is from the perspective of the preparers of accounting information (CPAs and others). The other is from the perspective of the users of that information. This text is primarily concerned with both the preparation and the use of accounting information.

* * * * *

Accounting poses as being exact. Not so. When you look at a firm's income statement and see the firm "earned" $2,561,500 last year and has total assets of $32,964,320, you get the impression that accounting is indeed rather precise. After all, the firm calculated income down to the hundreds of dollars and assets even more finely.

Accounting numbers, such as net income and total assets, are the result of a collection of arbitrary estimates, allocations and different accounting conventions. Let's illustrate. Assume our firm buys a $100,000 piece of equipment. We can take depreciation and allocate this cost over the equipment's expected useful life. How long is that useful life? Four years? Five? Six? Within limits, the decision as to how many years is up to us. Once we decide over how many years we want to spread the cost, we must then choose the method of depreciation we want to use. We can calculate an annual depreciation expense using the straight-line method or one of several different methods of accelerated depreciation. Any of the decisions we make will be equally acceptable, but each will result in different yearly expense and income levels and, subsequently, different asset values. Let's assume we have decided to depreciate the equipment over four years instead of five or six and that we estimate that it will have a salvage value of $10,000 at the end of four years.

In both cases we took a total of $90,000 in depreciation over the life of the asset, but along the way we had different depreciation expenses and different book values at the end of each year. And we could have depreciated the equipment over five or six years instead of four, resulting in yet different numbers.

At this point a person might ask why a company would pick one method over another. They do so in order to "manage" their income. In our example, the straight-line method resulted in constant depreciation expense over the four-year life of the asset. It also resulted in lower initial expenses and higher income than the declining-balance

Table I.1

	Straight-Line Depreciation		Declining-Balance Depreciation	
	Depreciation Expense	End-of-Year Book Value	Depreciation Expense	End-of-Year Book Value
	$	$	$	$
Year 1	22,500	77,500	50,000	50,000
Year 2	22,500	55,000	25,000	25,000
Year 3	22,500	32,500	12,500	12,500
Year 4	22,500	10,000	2,500	10,000
Total depreciation	90,000		90,000	

method provided. The declining-balance method results in lower income and hence lower income taxes during the first two years.

* * * * *

Here's another example: When a firm calculates the value of its inventory it can use several different methods, last-in-first-out (LIFO), first-in-first-out (FIFO), or a weighted average method. Again, these different methods will result in different costs, income and asset values.

Let's say we buy ten widgets for a dollar each ($10.00) on January 15 and eight widgets for $1.50 each ($12.00) on January 20. All widgets are identical and, when we buy them, we dump them into a bin along with what is already there. We now have 18 widgets which cost a total of $22.00. On January 30 we sell 15 widgets for $3.00 each. What was the cost of the widgets we sold and what was the cost of our inventory on January 31? It depends on which method of inventory valuation we used.

If we used LIFO to value our inventory, our cost was:

8 × $1.50 =	$12.00
7 × $1.00 =	$7.00
Total cost of goods sold	$19.00

The value of our ending inventory would be 3 units at $1 each or $3.00.

If we used FIFO, our cost was:

10 × $1.00 =	$10.00
5 × $1.50 =	$7.50
Total cost of goods sold	$17.50

The value of our ending inventory would be 3 units at $1.50 each or $4.50.

If we had used the weighted average method, the weighted average cost of our inventory would be $1.222 per unit ($22.00 ÷ 18 widgets). Consequently our cost of goods sold would be \$18.333 (15 units × \$1.222) and the value of our ending inventory would be \$3.666 (3 units × \$1.222). Three different methods, three different sets of values.

As an engineer once observed of accounting, "It's as though you measure with a micrometer, mark with a grease pencil and then cut with an axe." There's more than a little truth to his witticism.

It's important to realize, however, that the arbitrariness and inexactitude of accounting numbers do not necessarily render them less useful. Accounting numbers are really nothing more than reasonable estimates or approximations of real-world economic events. Furthermore, if we're talking about independently audited financial statements, it is reasonable to conclude that the assumptions and estimates on which the numbers rest were made in a consistent and conservative manner.

Terminology

A cautionary word about terminology. Accounting and finance terminology can sometimes be confusing to an experienced analyst, let alone a novice. This is because different authors use different terms to mean the same thing. For example, take the so-called "bottom line" on a firm's income statement. This is variously referred to as earnings, profit and/or net income. These are not to be confused with operating income, a very different concept. Owners' equity on one balance sheet (aka statement of change in financial position) might be referred to as stockholders' equity; it's also sometimes referred to simply as net worth. Or consider the number derived from subtracting a firm's cost of goods sold from its revenues. It is sometimes referred to as gross profit. On another income statement it might be listed as gross margin. These are not to be confused with contribution margin, which means something entirely different.

To add to the confusion, different writers and financial services sometimes use different formulas in calculating financial ratios such as return on assets. To overcome these potential problems, keep in mind the context in which a term is employed and be consistent in your own analysis.

Financial versus Managerial Accounting

Accounting can be segregated into two types – financial and managerial. The two have a lot in common, but their main differences lie in the fact that they have different audiences. Financial accounting is directed to users outside the firm – investors, creditors, suppliers and regulators. Publicly traded companies generally want this information to be widely circulated and easily obtained. Without available information, investors are not going to invest their funds, creditors will not make loans and suppliers will not provide much-needed credit. Furthermore, the Securities Exchange Commission (SEC) requires this information to be published. To see just how easily available this information is, do a quick Google search. Type the name of the publicly traded company in which you are interested along with "financial statements." You will instantly get their entire audited financial statements.

Managerial accounting, as the name implies, addresses the needs of management. The information needs of management are decidedly different than the needs of outside investors. Furthermore, this information is proprietary. Most companies don't want you or their competitors to know such things as their variable costs per unit, their breakeven point for different products, or their manufacturing overhead rates.

Financial accounting is regulated by the SEC and the Financial Accounting Standards Board (FASB). Together, they establish the rules for financial accounting. These rules are the so-called "Generally Accepted Accounting Principles" (GAAP). Other organizations such as the American Institute of Certified Public Accountants (AICPA), the Institute of Management Accountants (IMA) and the American Accounting Association (AAA) play a lesser role in establishing accounting principles, but the FASB and the SEC are the primary forces in the establishment of GAAP.

It's important for firms to follow GAAP for external reporting. To enable you, as a potential investor, to choose between investing in two or more different companies, the companies must all follow the same rules for measuring revenues, expenses, assets and liabilities.

Otherwise, you will have no basis for comparing their respective performances. It would be like comparing apples and oranges – or perhaps big apples and little apples. "Good" financial accounting, therefore, is that which consistently follows common rules laid forth by these two organizations.

Managerial accounting on the other hand is not regulated. A management accountant might say, "Rules? What rules? We don't need rules." And he or she would be right. The *sine qua non* of managerial accounting is simple: does it provide managers with the information they need to plan, organize, control and make good decisions? If it does, it's good. If it doesn't, it isn't. It's that simple. A well-designed accounting system provides good information, and good information leads to good decisions.

A common set of rules for management accounting, unlike financial accounting, doesn't make sense. Why so? The management of different types of companies have very different needs when it comes to information. The manager in a manufacturing firm will need different types of information than the manager in a department store, who in turn will need different information than a bank manager, and so on.

Summary

Accounting has been called the language of business. It follows then that those who pursue a career in business would do well to familiarize themselves with this language. To more fully understand business processes, it is useful to understand the language of business. It is important to realize that accounting numbers such as net income and total assets are not precise, but provide reasonable estimates and approximations of real-world economic events. Managers rely on these numbers when making decisions, planning, and controlling the operations of their organizations. Furthermore, their performance is often judged on the basis of accounting information.

One of the difficulties people often encounter with understanding accounting and finance literature is its terminology. Different authors use different terms to mean the same thing. Learning the language becomes the key. When coming across terms you might not understand, try to keep in mind the context in which they are used.

There are two major branches of accounting – financial and managerial. Each serves a distinct audience with different information needs. Financial accounting provides information to those outside the firm – investors, creditors, government regulatory agencies and the like. Managerial accounting provides information for managers and is the major thrust of this text.

1

THE BASICS

Chapter Overview

This chapter provides a description of the basic accounting framework. After studying this chapter, you will:

- Be aware of the different purposes accounting serves;
- Understand what an account is;
- Understand the difference between accrual and cash accounting;
- Know the two equations which underlie the income statement and balance sheet, respectively;
- Gain insight into a basic income statement, balance sheet, source and use of funds statement and a firm's operating cycle.

* * * * *

Accounting serves several purposes, all at the same time. The following are some examples:

1   **It's used to keep score.** It answers questions like "How are we doing?" Are we making a profit? If so, how much? Are we losing money? How is the West Coast division doing compared to the East Coast division?

2   **It directs attention to problems and opportunities.** Is our inventory getting too large? Is our product getting out

on time? Are we collecting our accounts in a timely fashion? What is happening to our profit margin?

3   **It provides information needed to control costs.** Before managers can control costs they need to know how much the costs are, how much the costs should be and what it is that causes them. A properly designed accounting system will provide this information.

4   **It provides information needed for planning.** Before managers can make plans they need to know how costs and profits react to changes in volume and production methods. For example, some costs will change proportionately with changes in production, some will change more than proportionately and some will not change at all.

5   **And it provides information for decision making.** Should we make this component ourselves or should we outsource it? Should we buy or lease a piece of equipment? Do we want to accept this special order at a price below our normal sales price? Again, a well-designed accounting system can provide a treasure trove of information that will help managers answer these kinds of questions.

* * * * *

To understand how to use accounting data, first understand that the basic accounting framework is an amazing system of recording, verifying, summarizing and reporting business transactions. It is truly a thing of beauty.

The most fundamental component of that framework is an account. An account is simply a device, a pigeonhole if you will, to logically order whatever it is we want to keep track of. Want to keep track of cash? Create a cash account. Want to keep track of inventory? How much people owe us? How much we owe others? How much are our sales? Our expenses? Create an account for each. Accounts can be created and destroyed at will. Maybe we sold a building. If so, close the building account and get rid of it.

Back in ancient times BC (before computer), creating or closing an account was as simple as putting a sheet of paper in or taking it out of a loose-leaf notebook. Today it can be as simple as creating or deleting a column in an Excel spreadsheet.

Modern accounting rests on a marvelous invention called double-entry bookkeeping. Double-entry bookkeeping is a method of recording every transaction an organization makes. Every transaction that a company makes will have an impact on two or more accounts. At least one account will be debited and at least one will be credited. And remember that debits will always equal credits.

Structurally, accounts are very simple. They have three parts: a title (what we're keeping track of), a left-hand side and a right-hand side. That's it. Period. We call the left-hand side the debit side and the right-hand side the credit side. When we debit an account, we simply make an entry on the left-hand side of the account. A credit is made on the right-hand side. Debit does *not* mean increase or decrease. It means left and that's all. Some accounts are increased when debited and some are decreased. The same holds true for credits. It all depends on the type of account. Sailors say "port and starboard." Accountants say "debit and credit." Below is an example of a "T" account.

There are five basic categories of accounts, with some variations thrown in to make it interesting. The five categories are: revenue, expense, asset, liability and owners' equity and, of course, there are many examples of each.

- Revenues are inflows of cash, increases in other assets or the settlement of liabilities resulting from the sale of goods and services that constitute an organization's principal operations.

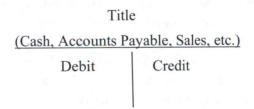

Title

(Cash, Accounts Payable, Sales, etc.)

Debit | Credit

Figure 1.1

- Expenses are the outflows of cash, the decreases in other assets or the incurrence of liabilities resulting from the performance of activities that constitute an organization's principal operations.
- Assets are the resources (tangible or intangible) which provide future economic benefit to their owner.
- Liabilities are the obligations of an organization to transfer assets or provide services to another entity.
- Owners' equity is the owners' claim to the net assets (assets minus liabilities) of an organization. There are two types of owners' equity accounts – paid-in capital and retained earnings.

Other accounts that might appear on an organization's accounting records are losses, gains and contra accounts. Gains and losses refer to the increase or decrease in an organization's assets and are the result of incidental transactions, not from events related to its principal operations. Contra accounts are sometimes referred to as evaluation accounts. They always accompany another account and are "contrary" to it. Fixed assets such as equipment or buildings will be accompanied by the contra account "accumulated depreciation."

Another example of a contra account is "allowance for doubtful accounts," which is contra to accounts receivable. It represents the difference between what an organization is owed and what it reasonably expects to receive.

Accrual Accounting

There is a specific point in a firm's operating cycle which represents *the* critical event in the revenue earning process. Usually that point is when a sale is made or a service is rendered, not when payment is received. Therefore, revenue is recorded when the sale is made or the service rendered. If the sale is on credit, an increase in accounts receivable (short-term asset) is also recorded. If it's a cash sale, then an increase in cash is recorded along with the sale. Note how the single transaction (a sale) had an impact on two accounts – sales and accounts receivable, or sales and cash.

Generally accepted accounting principles (GAAP) call for accountants to use accrual accounting for financial reporting. In accrual accounting, revenue is recorded when it's earned, not when payment is received. If a firm makes a sale on credit in December 2009 and is paid in January 2010, it records the revenue in 2009 and consequently 2009 income is affected. Likewise, expenses are recorded when they are incurred, not when they are paid.

Here's an example. Think of your favorite magazine. Assume that you paid $36 for a monthly, one-year subscription. When the publishing company received your check, it recorded an asset (cash) and a liability, or obligation, to provide you with a copy of the magazine each month for 12 months. The firm does not record revenue when it receives your payment because it has not yet been earned.

When the company sends your monthly copy of the magazine it reduces its liability by $3. It's at this point the firm recognizes $3 of revenue, because it has now been earned.

Cash Accounting

The counterpart to accrual accounting is cash accounting. Under the rules of cash accounting, revenue is recognized when cash is received and expenses are recognized when cash is paid. Before the days of Visa and MasterCard, doctors and dentists widely used cash accounting because of the uncertainty of receiving payment for their services. Today, you are probably not going to get further than the receptionist's desk without handing over your credit card. It's not surprising to learn that most doctors and dentists use accrual accounting today.

Equations

There are two very simple equations around which the accounting framework is built: the income equation: Revenues − Expenses = Profit; and the balance sheet equation: Assets = Liabilities + Owners' Equity.

Income Statement

Annual income twenty pounds, annual expenditure nineteen six, result happiness. Annual income twenty pounds, annual expenditure twenty pounds ought and six, result misery.

(Charles Dickens, David Copperfield, ch. 12)

Figures 1.2, 1.3 and 1.5 illustrate a typical income statement, balance sheet and source and use of funds statement respectively. Let's take a stroll through them.

Acme Corporation Income Statement For the Year Ended December 31 (000 omitted)	20X9	20X8
Revenues	$12,500	$11,800
Less Cost of Goods Sold	8,300	7,800
Gross Margin	4,200	4,000
Less: Selling, General and Admin. Expenses:		
Rent	630	670
Utilities	500	490
Insurance	400	380
Advertising	180	175
Depreciation	150	140
Research and Development	440	400
Operating Income	1,900	1,745
Other Income /Expense		
Interest Expense	620	650
Earnings before Tax	1,280	1,095
Income Tax	377	329
Earnings before Extraordinary Items	903	766
Extraordinary Loss (net of tax)	120	—
Net Income	$783	$766
(Dividends paid, $400)		
Common Stock Price	$58	$50

Figure 1.2

An income statement (Figure 1.2) can be likened to a movie. It tells a story about the firm's activities over a period of time. A firm's income statement tells the reader what the firm earned by selling its products or services, what activities it undertook to earn that revenue and how much those activities cost. Like some movies, it can have a happy ending; like others, it can be a horror show.

The opening scene, that is, the first item on the income statement, shows what the firm's revenues are, that is, what it earned from the sale of its principal products or services.

Cost of goods sold follows. If the company in question is a retail or wholesale firm, cost of goods sold represents the cost to the firm of the merchandise it sold plus all the related costs of transportation and taxes incurred to get the product on its shelves and out the door.

If the firm is a manufacturer, calculating cost of goods sold is considerably more complicated. It involves calculating the cost of materials and labor and estimating the overhead that went into manufacturing the firm's products. For a service firm, cost of services provided represents the labor and overhead expended to provide the firm's services.

Gross profit (aka gross margin) is a particularly important number on the income statement. Not only is it usually one of the larger amounts on the income statement, but it also represents the amount of money the firm has available to cover its selling and administrative expenses, interest and taxes and provide a return to the firm's owners. If gross profit is not adequate, the firm is not going to be profitable.

Selling and administrative expenses are obvious from their titles. Of those listed in our example, depreciation deserves special mention. Like other expenses, depreciation is a cost of doing business and is deducted from revenues to determine net income. Unlike other expenses, depreciation is a non-cash expense. That is, the firm writes a check and reduces its cash balance when it pays for wages, utilities and so on. It does not do so when it records depreciation.

Jump ahead for a moment and check out the balance sheet in Figure 1.3. Notice how accumulated depreciation reduces the amount reported for buildings and equipment. When the firm records depreciation expense it does not reduce cash or increase a liability; rather it reduces the book value of the asset being depreciated.

As we continue to move down the income statement (Figure 1.2), the next significant item is operating income. Don't confuse operating income with net income. Operating income is the income earned from *operating* the firm's assets. It is a measure of how effectively management has managed the assets with which they have been entrusted.

Note that "other income and expense" is listed after operating income. Interest expense and other non-operating income and expense items will always be shown in this section of the income statement. Interest expense is shown here because it is not an operating expense; it's a financing expense. To be successful, management must operate *and* finance the firm's assets effectively and efficiently.

We have now arrived at earnings before tax, also known as taxable income. You know what's coming next – federal, state and local income tax. Other taxes a company must pay are scattered throughout the income statement and balance sheet. Sales tax incurred on the firm's purchases will be included as part of the cost of inventory and materials in cost of goods sold, or as part of the cost of the equipment listed on the balance sheet. Property tax will be included as a component of manufacturing overhead, or selling, general and administrative expense.

After deducting income tax we generally arrive at net income. From time to time, however, something quite unusual might happen that leads to further gains or losses. In these cases, as in our example, the income statement will show gains or losses resulting from extraordinary items. In order to qualify for such treatment, the item in question must be *both* unusual and infrequent. Hurricane damage in New Orleans is not going to qualify, nor is tornado damage in Oklahoma City. Earthquake damage in North Dakota, however, might, because it would be highly unusual in this part of the United States.

Balance Sheet

In Figure 1.3 we can compare the Acme Corporation's financial position as of December 31, 20X9 with its financial position of December 31, 20X8.

Acme Corporation
Balance Sheet
As of December 31

(000 omitted)

	20X9	20X8
Assets		
Current Assets:		
Cash	$521	$298
Accounts Receivable	1,374	1,280
Inventory	2,236	2,310
Prepaid Items	150	120
Total Current Assets	4,281	4,008
Property, Plant and Equipment		
Buildings, Machinery and Trucks	3,600	3,500
Less Accumulated Depreciation	(1,200)	(1,050)
Net Prop., Plant and Equip.	2,400	2,450
Other Assets		
Long-Term Investments	1,500	1,400
Total Assets	$8,181	$7,858
Liabilities and Stockholders' Equity		
Current Liabilities:		
Accounts Payable	$920	$950
Wages Payable	850	805
Short-Term Notes Payable	345	320
Total Current Liabilities	2,115	2,075
Long-Term Debt	1,200	1,300
Owners' Equity		
Preferred Stock ($50 par, 6%, 1,000 sh. issued)	50	50
Common Stock ($8 par, 250,000 sh. issued)	2,000	2,000
Paid-in Capital in Excess of Par	500	500
Retained Earnings	2,316	1,933
Total Liabilities and Stockholders' Equity	$8,181	$7,858

Figure 1.3

Assets, unfortunately, do not fall from heaven like manna. They have to be financed. The right-hand side of the balance sheet equation (Assets = Liabilities + Owners' Equity) lists the sources of the firm's financing. There are two general types of financing: debt equity and owners' equity.

The balance sheet equation merely states that a firm's assets have to equal the ownership claims to those assets. As an equation, both sides have to be equal. If they aren't, something is wrong. The value of a firm's assets always has to equal the value of the firm's liabilities and owners' equity.

If the income statement can be compared to a movie, the balance sheet can be compared to a photograph. The balance sheet provides the reader with a financial snapshot. It shows what the firm's resources (i.e. assets) and its liabilities and owners' equity are as of the close of business on a specific date. For a firm's annual report, that date will be the last day of its fiscal year. The financial snapshot can reveal a pretty picture or show a disaster.

A well-run firm will have the right amount of the right assets at the right time to carry on its activities. Too many assets represent wasted investments. Machinery sitting idle and collecting dust is not a good thing; neither is excessive inventory sitting in a warehouse or on the car lot. On the other hand, a firm needs adequate resources if it is to grow or even sustain its current level of operations.

As the name implies, debt equity (i.e. liabilities) represents what the firm owes. These debts take various forms: accounts payable, accrued wages payable, both short- and long-term notes payable, and interest payable are common examples. The difference between short-term and long-term liabilities is due to timing. Short-term liabilities are expected to be settled within the coming year.

Owners' equity represents the owners' financial interests in the firm's assets. The total amount of owners' equity is the result of how much owners have invested in the firm, either through a direct contribution (stock purchase, etc.) or through the firm's earnings that have been kept (retained) in the business and not paid out to the owners in the form of dividends or other payments.

If the firm has suffered sizable losses over time, owners' equity could be negative. In this unhappy situation, liabilities would be greater than assets and the future of the firm could be in question.

Assets

As we review the assets on the balance sheet of the Acme Corporation, the first heading we encounter is current assets. Current assets are cash and other assets which will either be used up or turned into cash within one operating cycle or one year, whichever is longer. An operating cycle is how long it takes a firm to go from a cash-to-cash position. More specifically, it is that period of time from when a firm purchases inventory until it receives cash from making a sale.

Figure 1.4 represents a typical operating cycle for a manufacturing firm. Operating cycles for different firms vary dramatically. For a firm like a McDonald's restaurant, the operating cycle is probably (hopefully) a couple of days at most. For the maker of ocean liners or the builder of high-rise condos it might be several years.

Current assets are listed in the order of their liquidity. By liquidity we mean how readily these assets can be turned into cash. Jumping ahead for a bit, note that Acme Corporation's cash increased from $298 to $521 during 20X9 (an increase of $223). The source and use of funds statement for 20X9 will show what activities took place that led to that increase. We'll explore that useful statement shortly.

Figure 1.4

Accounts receivable, perhaps surprisingly, does not necessarily show what customers owe us. What it does show is how much we expect to receive from them. The ugly truth is that not everyone who buys on credit pays. If the bulk of our sales is on credit and if we have a history of having, let's say, 2 percent of our sales go uncollected, we need to reflect that fact by reducing the amount of accounts receivable shown on the balance sheet. Some of the debt owed to us is just not going to be received.

Inventory can be shown at different amounts depending on whether we value it on a first-in-first-out (FIFO), last-in-first-out (LIFO) or weighted average basis. Here is a way to keep these terms straight. The next time you go to the grocery store and buy a carton of milk, think FIFO. The stockperson always puts the oldest milk in front. They don't want you rooting around buying the freshest, most recently purchased. They want the first milk purchased to be the first milk sold. When you think of LIFO, think of a barrel of nails. When you go to the hardware store, you are not going to dig down to the bottom of the barrel to get the oldest nails. You will gingerly take a handful from the top. That is, the last ones put in the barrel will be the first ones sold. The gas station gives a good notion of weighted average. The ten gallons you just put in your car's tank cannot be distinguished from any other ten gallons in the station's inventory.

When accountants use terms like FIFO, LIFO or weighted average, they are only talking about the flow of costs, not the physical flow of goods. The actual inventory might consist of newly purchased items, yet carry costs of inventory that came and went a long time ago. A fishmonger could use LIFO to value his inventory. If he actually sold fish on a last-in-first-out basis, his remaining inventory could be pretty old.

Using LIFO results in the most recent costs of inventory being matched against current revenues – a good measure of profit. However, in a period of inflation it also results in the amount of inventory reported on the balance sheet being old, possibly outdated costs.

Using FIFO results in just the opposite: the firm will be matching older costs against current revenues, which could possibly distort income. The balance sheet, however, will report current values. The use of a weighted average to value inventory results in an averaging of old and new costs in inventory and the cost of goods sold.

Also, inventory should be shown on the balance sheet at the lower-of-cost-or-market. That is, if the value for which we can sell it has fallen below our initial cost, we should "write down" the value of the inventory to reflect that fact. If we bought inventory for $100 and can now sell it for only $80, we need to show a loss on the income statement and the lower value on the balance sheet. Otherwise we will misrepresent the value of inventory and the value of the firm.

The next heading on the balance sheet is property, plant and equipment (PP&E). These assets are reported at their original cost less any depreciation taken to date, that is, accumulated depreciation. Their reported values do not necessarily reflect current market values. If a firm purchased a building ten years ago for $200,000, depending on where it was located it might today have a value of $300,000 or $400,000 or more. On the balance sheet, however, it would reflect a value of less than $200,000 – its original cost minus accumulated depreciation.

Some critics see the practice of reporting asset values at their original cost less accumulated depreciation as an over-reliance on the so-called principle of objectivity. They point to it as an example of objectivity trumping usefulness. Others argue that market estimates are inherently subjective and should not be used. Whichever side of the issue one comes down on, it is clear that if there is a substantial difference between original cost and current market value of PP&E an obvious problem exists for anyone wanting to determine the value or financial health of a company by analyzing its financial statements. This is particularly true if PP&E constitutes a significant amount of the firm's assets.

Take a moment to compare the 20X8 and 20X9 figures for Acme Corporation's PP&E (Figure 1.3). The firm purchased $100 of building, machinery or trucks during the year, yet the net amount of PP&E was reduced by $50. This is because the firm reported $150 in depreciation expense. You can confirm this by looking at Acme's income statement (Figure 1.2). In other words, Acme depreciated property, plant and equipment by more than they purchased during 20X9, causing its net book value to decrease.

The income statement shows how much depreciation was taken during the current year. The account, accumulated depreciation, shows the total amount of depreciation that has accumulated (been taken) on the firm's assets over time.

As long as an asset is being used, even if it is fully depreciated and has a book value of zero, it, along with the accompanying accumulated depreciation account, should remain on the company's books. This informs the reader that the firm still has and is using the particular asset, but that it has been fully depreciated. When the asset is retired, the asset account and its accompanying contra account should be removed from the balance sheet.

The last section under assets on Acme's balance sheet is other assets. This is basically a catchall heading. It's where a firm lists those assets that don't fit in the categories above and generally includes non-operating assets. In Acme's case we find long-term investments. These are investments in financial securities of some sort, possibly an investment in a government bond or another firm's preferred or common stock or long-term bonds.

Other assets that might be listed here include intangible assets such as copyrights, patents or goodwill. Intangible assets have no physical qualities. You can't hold, touch, smell or paint them but they are nevertheless very real and often very valuable. Their value comes from the fact that they give the firm some right or advantage that other firms do not have. For example, they might give their owner the exclusive right to publish a book or use a certain trademark.

Goodwill is the most intangible of intangibles. It will appear on a firm's balance sheet only when that firm has purchased another firm and paid more for it than the market value of its individual assets. Goodwill can be thought of as representing the superior earning power of the purchased firm's assets.

Liabilities and Stockholders' Equity

Moving over to the other side of the balance sheet we find the sources of financing for the firm's assets, that is, liabilities and stockholders' equity.

Current liabilities are always listed first. These liabilities generally arise from the normal course of day-to-day business. As their name implies, they are short-term liabilities that will be paid from current assets. They generally include such items as accounts payable, which most often arise from credit purchases of inventory and supplies, and from accruals, which are liabilities that have grown with the passage of time but have not yet been paid. Examples of accruals include wages earned by employees but not yet paid and interest that has accrued on loans.

Long-term debt is debt that has a maturity date somewhere off in the future – usually a year or more – and that will not be paid from current assets. It will often be re-financed through additional long-term borrowing or paid by liquidating specific assets. For example, the firm might establish a special fund into which they make periodic deposits in order to retire the debt when it matures. If a firm has long-term debt, specific information regarding interest rates, maturity dates and pledged assets (if any) will be disclosed in the notes to the financial statements which accompany the financial statements.

The notes are an important part of a firm's annual report. They disclose important information that doesn't fit in the highly structured statements. We'll discuss them towards the end of this chapter.

We have now arrived at the owners' equity section of the balance sheet. The only difference in accounting for a proprietorship, partnership or corporation is in accounting for owners' equity. In our example, the Acme company is a corporation.

There are two ways in which the owners' equity in a company (corporate or otherwise) can be increased: through a direct contribution of assets to the company and through the company's earnings. In a proprietorship, there is only one owner and only one owner's equity account, Joan Doe – Capital. Both her contribution of assets to the company and the company's earnings that she has not withdrawn for personal use are combined in the capital account. Looking at the capital account for a proprietor you cannot tell how much of the capital comes from her contribution of assets and how much comes from the firm's earnings that have not been withdrawn.

In a partnership, there is a separate account for each owner, although on the financial statement these individual accounts will probably be combined into one. (Large accounting and law firms might have dozens or even hundreds of partners.)

Accounting for corporations is more complicated because their financing is more complicated. In our example, Acme has four different owners' equity accounts. Common stock is the basic ownership unit of a corporation. It carries with it all the basic rights of ownership: the right to vote in elections for membership on the board of directors, the right to residual profits, the right to residual assets in the event the corporation is liquidated and also the inalienable right to suffer losses.

Preferred stock is an interesting animal; it is neither fish nor fowl. That is, it is not a liability, nor does it represent ownership rights in the usual sense of the word. It's a bit of a hybrid. Generally, a preferred stockholder has neither the protection the law accords holders of debt nor the rights held by common stockholders. Yet it has elements of both. In a worst-case scenario when a corporation has to declare bankruptcy and liquidate, preferred stockholders' claims to the assets will come after the debt holders but before the common stockholders. Also, while preferred stock dividends are not guaranteed, preferred stockholders will receive dividends before common stockholders. Thus, preferred stockholders are in a *preferred* position when it comes to the distribution of dividends and assets.

Both preferred and common stock may or may not have a stated par value. Par value is an arbitrary value given to the stock when the firm incorporates. It is a relic from the past and bears no relationship to a stock's current market value. Some states do not require a corporation to declare a par value; others do. In those cases where a corporation's stock carries a par value, the stock must be recorded on the books at par value. In our example, Acme Corporation's common stock has a par value of $8 per share. The stock, however, initially sold at $10 per share. The extra $2 per share is recorded as paid-in capital in excess of par. Acme's preferred stock has a par value of $50 and pays an annual dividend of 6 percent of par, that is, $3 per share.

The final item on the balance sheet to consider is retained earnings. Retained earnings are ethereal. Reviewing the balance sheet, all of the items we've mentioned so far are fairly easy to visualize: We need only refer to our checkbook and monthly bank statements to visualize cash in the bank; accounts receivable can be visualized as a stack of invoices showing what customers owe us; we can see the inventory piled on shelves or stored in the warehouse; buildings and machinery are obvious. We can even visualize intangible assets like copyrights and patents by the legal document which gives evidence to them. On the equity side of the balance sheet, accounts payable are represented by invoices showing what we owe our suppliers; long-term debt is represented by a signed note; preferred and common stock is represented by stock certificates. But what about retained earnings? What are they? There's nothing to hold in your hand; there's nothing to paint, nothing to box or bind. There is nothing to visualize.

Retained earnings are simply earnings that have been retained in the company instead of being paid out to the owners. Retained earnings are the stockholders' claim to assets from profitable operations.

Where have these earnings gone? What's been done with them? The answer is, just about everything. They could have been used to buy buildings and inventory, to pay for research and development, to pay off creditors, to increase cash or to finance their customers' purchases. Retained earnings merely represent the amount by which the book value of assets exceeds all the other claims to the assets. That's all they are.

Source and Use of Funds Statement

Cash flow is the lifeblood of any company. Without adequate cash, a company cannot continue operations. It becomes illiquid. It cannot pay its expenses or its debts, or buy the assets it needs to operate. History is full of examples of profitable companies that were brought to their knees because they could not generate the cash necessary to carry on their business.

The source and use of funds statement (Figure 1.5) (aka cash flow statement) provides a unique insight into the company and

Acme Corporation
Source and Use of Funds Statement
For the Year Ended December 31, 20X9

(000 omitted)

Cash at Beginning of Year	$298
Net Cash from Operations:	
Net Income	$783
Plus Depreciation	150
Plus Reduction in Inventory	74
Less Increase in Accounts Receivable	(94)
Less Increase in Prepaid Items	(30)
Less Decrease in Accounts Payable	(30)
Plus Increase in Wages Payable	45
Plus Increase in Short-Term Notes Payable	25
	923
Net Cash from Investing Activities:	
Purchase of Building, Machinery and Trucks	(100)
Purchase of Long-Term Investment	(100)
	(200)
Net Cash from Financing Activities:	
Payment of Long-Term Debt	(100)
Payment of Dividends	(400)
	500
Net Change in Cash	$223
Cash at End of Year	$521

Figure 1.5

management's philosophy that the other two statements do not. Specifically, the statement shows where the firm's cash came from and what the firm did with it. The statement lists three sources and uses of cash – operating activities, investing activities and financing activities.

Net cash from operations is different than income from operations for two basic reasons: (1) some revenue and expense items do not involve cash (depreciation is an example); and (2) there is often a difference between the time a firm recognizes a revenue or expense and the time it receives or spends cash. For example, a sale might be made on credit in December and the payment not received until January. Likewise, December's utility expense might not be paid until January. This section of the source and use of funds statement in essence reconciles operating income and cash received from operations.

To calculate cash received from operations, start with net income and then add any non-cash expenses such as depreciation. Next, add reductions in other current assets and increases in current liabilities. Then deduct decreases in current liabilities and increases in current assets. The logic in this is not always clear at first. It can seem a bit counterintuitive until you get the hang of it. Perhaps a couple of examples will help.

Consider accounts receivable. If a firm's accounts receivable balance increases during the year, it indicates that customers bought more on credit than they paid on their existing balances. Since credit sales are included in net income, sales would be greater than the amount of cash collected. Consequently, to arrive at cash received from sales we need to deduct the amount of increase in accounts receivable.

Let's illustrate that last point by referring to the Acme Corporation's financial statements. During 20X9 Acme had revenues of $12,500,000. Also during the year their accounts receivable increased from $1,280,000 to $1,374,000. This is an increase of $94,000 and represents earnings that have not been collected. If we want to determine the cash received from operations we will have to deduct the $94,000.

Here's another example. If inventory levels increase during a period of time it means we bought more inventory than we sold; that is, we bought more than we charged against income in the form of cost of goods sold. To go from net income to cash provided by operations, we need to subtract the amount of the increase in inventory. Conversely, if inventory levels declined during the year, then we expensed more than we spent for inventory. In this case we would need to add back the amount of the reduction in inventory. It's tricky, but, if you stop and think about it, it becomes clear. The logic is similar for other current assets and liabilities as well.

It's not uncommon for a start-up firm to have a negative cash flow from operations. As its credit sales and accounts receivable increase and as it buys additional inventory to satisfy growing demand, the cash the firm receives from sales might not be sufficient to finance this growth. For a more mature company, however, cash flow from operations should be positive. If cash flows continue to be negative, it probably means the firm will need to find additional outside financing. If this situation continues, the time will come when the firm will not be able to service its debt and continue operations. This is not a good thing.

Net cash from investing activities involves buying and selling non-current assets. When a firm buys these assets the transaction is shown in this section as a use of cash; when it sells non-current assets the transaction represents a source of cash. In the Acme Corporation example, the firm purchased machinery for $100,000 and made a long-term investment of $100,000. Once again, note how the financial statements are related and that these purchases are also reflected on the balance sheet as increases in the value of these two assets.

Normally, we would expect net cash from investing activities to reflect a net use of cash. As long as the firm is growing, or even maintaining its current level of assets by replacing old buildings and equipment, this section will show a net use of cash. In any given year a firm may, of course, sell off some assets for any number of reasons. If, however, this section of the statement shows a net source of cash over a period of time, it probably means a firm is downsizing or perhaps even liquidating.

Net cash from financing activities refers to long-term financing. Incurring long-term debt and selling preferred or common stock are sources of funds from financing activities. The payment of long-term debt and dividends and the purchase of a firm's own stock are examples of uses of funds.

* * * * *

Think of the chain and sprocket on a bicycle. The teeth of the sprocket fit precisely in the spaces on the chain. They work in harmony. What happens to one affects the other. So it is with a firm's income statement, balance sheet and source and use of funds statement. Whatever happens on the income statement affects the balance sheet and the source and use of funds statement and vice versa.

Let's examine how the three financial statements are related. Begin with Acme's income statement on page 14. Note that net income is $783,000 and that dividends of $400,000 were paid. Consequently, $383,000 of earnings were not paid out to stockholders; they were retained. Now check out the balance sheet on page 17. Note the increase in retained earnings from 20X8 to 20X9 – once again, $383,000. Retained earnings are the linchpin that connects the income statement and the balance sheet. Retained earnings are the cumulative result of all operating and financing decisions and transactions (including the payment of dividends) the company has made since the day it opened for business.

The source and use of funds statement incorporates data from both of the other statements. This statement reports the impact on cash of all the operating and financing decisions and transactions of the firm during the past year. Once again, look at the balance sheet. Note that cash increased from $298,000 in 20X8 to $521,000 in 20X9, an increase of $223,000. What activities caused that increase? An examination of the source and use of funds statement reveals the answer.

Footnotes to Financial Statements

We earlier alluded to the notes to the financial statements. The whole purpose of creating financial statements is to give the reader as complete and accurate a picture of the firm as possible. The raison d'être of accounting is to provide useful economic information. The basic framework of accounting – the accounts and the rules of debit and credit – has limitations. To give the reader a better picture of the economics of the firm, accountants need to provide additional information. They do so in the form of footnotes. These footnotes

will summarize significant accounting policies. (Did the firm use
LIFO or FIFO to value inventory? What method of depreciation was
used? And so on.) The footnotes will also provide other information,
such as detailed information about investments, contract provisions,
employee retirement plans and pending lawsuits, that is relevant to
understanding the firm's financial position. To illustrate their significance, look at Columbia Sportswear's financial statements in Appendix A. The income statement, balance sheet and statement of cash
flows are accompanied by 17 footnotes.

Summary

Accounting provides information for a number of purposes: (1) keeping score of how well the organization is doing; (2) directing managers' attention to problems and opportunities; (3) controlling costs; (4)
planning and (5) decision making.

The most fundamental component of an accounting system is
an account, which is a very simple device that has three parts: the
title of what we want to keep track of; a left-hand side (debit); and a
right-hand side (credit). Accounting systems have five major types of
accounts: revenues, expenses, assets, liabilities and owners' equity.

Double-entry accounting is based on two simple equations. The
income equation: Revenues − Expenses = Net Income; and the balance sheet equation: Assets = Liabilities + Owners' Equity.

The chapter discusses the difference between accrual and cash
accounting. Accrual accounting, the generally accepted method
for public corporations, records revenues when they are earned as
opposed to when they are received and expenses as they are incurred
as opposed to when they are paid. Cash accounting records revenues
when received and expenses when paid.

This chapter illustrates and provides a detailed discussion of the
three major accounting statements: the income statement, the balance sheet and the source and use of funds statement. It also demonstrates how those three statements are related. A change in any one
of them will result in changes in the other two.

Exercises

1 List the type of account (asset, liability, owners' equity, revenue, expense) and the financial statement on which it belongs for the following:

Account	Type	Financial Statement
Cash		
Depreciation expense		
Accumulated depreciation		
Accounts receivable		
Accounts payable		
Dividends		
Prepaid rent		
Utilities expense		
Inventory		
Employee wages		
Income tax		
Interest payable		

2 Calculate the missing amounts for each firm.

Table 1.1

	Firm X	Firm Y	Firm Z
Total assets 12/31/11	$500,000		$350,000
Total liabilities 12/31/11	200,000	450,000	
Paid-in capital 12/31/11	30,000	100,000	50,000
Retained earnings 12/31/11			125,000
Net income for 2011	80,000	120,000	150,000
Dividends paid in 2011	30,000	50,000	
Retained earnings 12/31/10		180,000	90,000

3 A prankster arranged Proctor Company's ledger accounts in alphabetical order. Note that the retained earnings account balance is for January 1, 20X9. All revenue and expense accounts are for the year 20X9.

Accounts payable	$20,000
Accounts receivable	12,000
Accumulated depreciation	40,000
Cash	70,000
Common stock (10,000 shares)	100,000
Cost of goods sold	130,000
Dividends paid during 20X9	28,000
Equipment	130,000
Income tax expense	12,000
Interest expense	5,000
Inventory	42,000
Long-term debt	40,000
Retained earnings 1/1/X9	21,000
Sales	250,000
Selling and administrative expenses	42,000

Prepare an income statement for 20X9 and a balance sheet for Proctor Company as of December 31, 20X9.

2

COSTS, COST BEHAVIOR AND COST ANALYSIS

Which of you, intending to build a tower, sitteth not down first, and counteth the cost, whether he have sufficient to finish it?

(Luke 14:28)

Chapter Overview

This chapter discusses various cost concepts and the notion that different costs are appropriate for different purposes. After studying this chapter, you will:

- Understand that the term "cost" has different meanings
- Realize that costs relevant for one decision may not be relevant for another
- Understand the difference between fixed, variable, mixed and discretionary costs
- Understand the meaning of sunk costs and their limited usefulness in decision making
- Understand the difference between direct and indirect costs
- Understand the difference between expired and unexpired costs

* * * * *

Increased global commerce, brought about by advances in production, communication and transportation technologies as well as relative worldwide political stability, has led to an increase in global economic competition. As a result of this increase in competition, cost control is more important than ever. Firms cannot compete on the basis of price alone.

In a market environment where there is little competition, firms are able to raise or lower prices without worrying too much about what their competition is going to do. In a competitive marketplace, however, where comparable goods are readily available, a firm doesn't have that ability. Why not? If a firm increases prices in a competitive market and its competitors do not, it will lose sales. Hondas, Toyotas and Fords are not perfect substitutes for one another, but they're pretty good substitutes. If Honda increases the price of its cars while Toyota and Ford do not, Honda will most likely lose market share. Honda managers also know that if they lower the price of the Accord or Civic their competitors will likely do the same with their cars. The other manufacturers are going to battle for market share. If one lowers its price and the others follow suit, everyone winds up with relatively the same market share but lower profit margins.

Because cost control is essential for success in such an environment, one needs to know what costs are, what causes them and how they behave.

The standard definition of "cost" as the amount of assets given up or the liabilities incurred in order to acquire some good or service is fine as far as it goes, but is too narrow to encompass the many different concepts of cost. The familiar refrain "Different strokes for different folks" is applicable for our discussion. Let's modify this to: Financial decision making utilizes different costs for different purposes. A cost that is relevant for one purpose may not be relevant for another.

Cost Classifications

Costs can be classified in a host of different ways. They can be classified as being **expired** or **unexpired**. An **expired cost** is an expense. For example, advertising expense is the cost of advertising that we did in the past. Maintenance expenses for last July are the costs we incurred for maintenance services last July. Rent expense is the cost of having used the office. These all represent costs that were incurred for a service that has expired.

Unexpired costs are assets. Assets represent stored-up services. As those services are used, the cost of the asset becomes an expense of doing business. Equipment represents future production capability. Inventory represents the cost of future sales. A building represents future shelter, and so on. Consequently, many assets can be thought of as expenses waiting to happen. (Cash, accounts receivable, marketable securities and land are exceptions.)

As buildings and equipment are used, their book values are reduced when the firm records depreciation expense. When inventory is sold, its value is reduced by the amount charged to cost of goods sold.

Costs can also be classified by the way they behave in relation to changes in output or other factors. We can classify most costs as variable, fixed or mixed. In the short-short run, the majority of costs firms face are fixed. As time goes by firms have greater and greater opportunities to change their cost structure and control the behavior of costs. For example, most firms probably cannot do much about the size of their workforce or productive capacity for the next week or so. Over the next several months, however, these firms can increase or decrease their workforce and increase or decrease their production capacity.

A **variable cost** is one that varies *in total* with output. The perfect example of a variable cost is direct materials. If we increase production, say, 10 percent, we will use 10 percent more materials and our materials costs will increase accordingly, assuming, of course, a constant rate of usage and a constant cost per unit of materials.

Fixed costs are sometimes referred to as capacity costs because most fixed costs relate to capacity. The larger the manufacturing plant or the larger the retail store, the greater the fixed costs such as depreciation, rent, taxes and insurance.

The term "relevant range" is somewhat of a misnomer, but nevertheless it refers to that range of activity over which a firm expects fixed costs to be consistent. By definition, fixed costs remain fixed within the relevant range. However, as we increase production beyond the upper limit of this range we will run out of room and max out the capacity of our equipment. We will need to increase the size of our plant and buy more machinery. This in turn will increase the costs related to these assets which were fixed at a lower level.

Within the relevant range, however, some costs will remain fixed regardless of whether we produce near the lower or upper end. If the rent on our factory is $10,000 per month, our landlord is not going to care whether we produce 100 widgets or 10,000 or if we go on vacation and produce none. The landlord is going to want the $10,000 every month.

Utilities and your cell phone bill are good examples of **mixed costs** – costs that have both a fixed and a variable element. If we turn off the lights, close the plant down and go on vacation, we will have a bill from the local electric utility company waiting for us when we get back. That's the fixed portion. It's a monthly charge which allows for a limited number of kilowatt hours and for being hooked up to the power grid. After we use the predetermined number of kilowatts, we'll start being charged so much per additional kilowatt we use – the variable portion. Likewise, many cell phone contracts allow you to use a given number of minutes per month at a set fee; after you've used those minutes you're charged a certain amount per minute for further usage.

Other costs vary, not with output, but with other production activities. If a factory produces different products or even different models of the same product, management will often have to stop production for a period of time while it sets the equipment to manufacture the new product or model. When it does, it will incur setup costs. These costs do not vary with the number of units it produces but with the number of batches it runs. It may be stating the obvious to point out that a firm can reduce these costs by making larger production runs of each product. The flip side, however, is that by producing more units it will incur higher inventory management costs.

Firms pursuing a just-in-time (JIT) inventory policy generally produce in smaller batches. These firms find that other advantages afforded by a JIT policy offset the higher setup costs. As with most decisions a manager must face there are trade-offs that need to be taken into account.

Costs may also vary with the number and complexity of different products and models a firm produces. These are generally engineering-related costs. Back in the day when Henry Ford was making Model Ts and promising customers they could have any color they wanted as long as it was black, he did not need a lot of engineers, particularly when he only made one basic model and then produced that same model for several years. Consider Ford Motor Company today with its myriad models and makes and how often these models get changed. Think about how much more complicated cars are today than they were when they were competing with horses for a lane. It's pretty easy to see that Ford has considerably greater engineering costs today than Henry did 90 years ago.

Discretionary costs are in a category all by themselves. The amount and timing of these costs are completely at management's discretion, hence the name. Research and development, advertising, preventive maintenance and management training are examples. In any given period, management might decide to spend heavily or defer these costs to a later period.

Sunk cost is a particularly apt term; think *Titanic*. Sunk costs are costs that have been incurred and, no matter what we do, we're not going to get them back. They're gone. They are historical and largely irrelevant to most decisions we might make. The problem with sunk costs is that managers often do not realize they are irrelevant and try to factor them into their decision models.

You've probably heard someone say, "We've got X amount of money tied up in that thing and we need to sell it for enough to get our money back." What they have is a sunk cost on their hand and they're trying to use it to make a marketing decision. Bad choice. The amount they have "tied up in it" is irrelevant. What is relevant is the market value of whatever it is they're trying to sell. This seems obvious, but sometimes it can be a hard rule to follow.

We can also classify costs as product costs or period costs. The distinction is important in determining profits and asset values. As the name implies, **product costs** attach to the products a company manufactures. These include the costs of the materials, labor and overhead that go into the product. The important point is that, regardless of when they are incurred, product costs are not matched against revenue in determining net income until the product is sold. A product might be manufactured one year and sold the next. If that's the case, the costs incurred will be considered an asset (inventory) until the item is sold and then it will be charged to cost of goods sold and deducted from sales. On the other hand, **period costs** are regarded as expenses and matched against revenue in the period in which they are incurred.

Costs can be classified as being direct or indirect. A **direct cost** is one that can be traced directly to a cost object, that is, the object for which we are trying to find the cost. A cost object could be a product that we manufacture, a service we provide, a unit within the organization such as the maintenance department, or a period of time. Materials are an example of a direct cost of a product. If we're making chairs and desks, we can measure the wood that goes into a chair and trace its cost directly back to the invoice. The maintenance guy's salary is a direct cost of the maintenance department. Last month's utility costs can be traced directly back to a specific period of time. These latter two costs, however, are indirect with respect to the products.

Indirect costs are very much a cost of a product; they just can't be traced directly to it. In every product we produce and every service we provide there are overhead costs, but how much depreciation, utilities, taxes or insurance is in that chair we manufactured? We simply cannot tell for certain. Therefore, we have to find a way to allocate a certain amount of these indirect costs to our various products.

One of the most important functions of accounting is to provide management with reliable and useful cost information. One of the most important types of costs management must consider when making decisions is opportunity costs. What are **opportunity costs** and where are they found in the accounting records? The standard definition of opportunity costs is the forgone value of the best alternative. Economists are fond of saying, "There's no such thing as a free lunch." What they mean is, no matter what we do, we have to give up something else in order to do it. They're talking about opportunity costs. If we choose a particular course of action, it excludes the possibility of some other action. The value or benefit from the forgone action is our opportunity cost. If we choose to produce desks today and not produce chairs, the contribution lost from not making the chairs is our opportunity cost. If a friend took you to lunch and picked up the tab you wouldn't have been able to spend that time reading this chapter.

Clearly, it is important that we consider opportunity costs when making decisions. So where do we find these all-important costs in the accounting records? We don't. Opportunity costs represent would-be benefits from transactions that never occurred. Consequently they are not recorded and do not appear in the accounting records.

We can, however, use accounting information to estimate what these costs might be. For example, we can estimate what the opportunity cost of buying versus making a component part or of accepting versus not accepting an order below the full cost of our product might be.

We have listed a number of different ways in which costs can be classified. Any given cost will fit in two or more of the categories we've mentioned. For example, in one situation labor could be a direct variable product cost. In a different firm under different conditions labor could be considered an indirect fixed cost. Maintenance can be categorized as an indirect discretionary product cost. In another situation it could be considered as a period cost. The particular set of circumstances and decision we face will dictate how a given cost should be categorized.

When analyzing costs for decision-making or control purposes we should keep in mind the cost driver. That is what causes the cost to be what it is. We'll take this subject up in Chapter 8.

Summary

This chapter discusses the importance of cost control in a competitive market. It differentiates expired from unexpired costs; variable from fixed and mixed costs; and direct from indirect costs. It defines discretionary, sunk, product, period and opportunity costs. This chapter also discusses the fact that costs relevant for one decision may not be relevant for another and that costs relevant for decision making may not be useful for planning or cost control making.

Exercises

1   Adam, a chef, left his $35,000-a-year job to start his own restaurant. Adam now draws a salary of $20,000. Identify his opportunity costs. Identify his opportunity costs if he had not left his prior job.
2   What is the difference between an expense and a cost?
3   Define the following terms: sunk cost, variable cost, product cost, period cost.

3

COST-VOLUME-PROFIT ANALYSIS

Chapter Overview

This chapter discusses different cost behavior patterns, their impact on operating income, the computation of a firm's breakeven point and operating leverage. After studying this chapter you will be able to:

- Understand the difference between traditional and contribution margin income statements;
- Understand the mathematics of the basic cost-volume-profit model;
- Identify the assumptions inherent in cost-volume-profit analysis;
- Calculate a company's breakeven point;
- Perform sensitivity analysis for different marketing and operating decisions;
- Understand the impact of operating leverage on a firm's operating profit.

* * * * *

Cost-volume-profit (C-V-P) analysis is one of the most useful tools in any manager's toolbox. It provides information and insights necessary for effective planning, budgeting and decision making.

In Chapter 2 we defined variable and fixed costs. The cost of direct materials was cited as a good example of variable costs. If we increase output by 10 percent, we will use 10 percent more material; hence our cost for materials will increase proportionately. We used rent as an example of a fixed cost. Our landlord is indifferent as to whether we produce many or few products, but wants the monthly rent payment regardless of our production.

Contribution margin is defined as the difference between revenues and variable costs. Contribution margin can be calculated on a per-unit basis (sales price minus variable cost per unit) or a total basis (total sales less total variable costs). These definitions are important for an understanding of C-V-P analysis.

Let's begin our discussion of C-V-P analysis by comparing two different income statements built on the same revenues and costs.

Contribution Margin versus Traditional Income Statements

In Figure 3.1, both income statements show revenues of $10,000, total costs of $8,500 and net income of $1,500. They serve different

---

Traditional Income Statement

Sales	$10,000
Less Cost of Goods Sold	6,000
Gross Profit	$4,000
Less Selling, General and Admin. Expense	2,500
Net Income	$1,500

Contribution Margin Income Statement

Sales	$10,000
Less Variable Costs:	
Manufacturing	$4,000
Sell, Gen. and Admin.	1,500
Total Variable Costs	5,500
Contribution Margin	$4,500
Less Fixed Costs:	
Manufacturing	$2,000
Sell, Gen. and Admin.	1,000
Total Fixed Costs	3,000
Net Income	$1,500

Figure 3.1

purposes, however. The traditional approach is prepared for external financial reporting, and it serves this purpose well. It draws readers' attention to the costs of different functions (i.e. cost of goods sold and selling, general and administrative expenses). This is the kind of information investors, creditors and government bureaucrats want.

The traditional approach, however, does not provide the information a person needs to make operating and marketing decisions because it lumps together both fixed and variable costs. As presented in the traditional income statement, cost of goods sold includes both fixed and variable costs, as do selling, general and administrative expenses. If this was the only information available and you wanted to know the impact on profits if sales volume was to increase or decrease by, say, 10 percent, what could you determine? Nothing. You wouldn't know how much of your costs was fixed and how much was variable. You would be unable to determine what the impact of a change in volume would be with any degree of accuracy. Remember, bad information is worse than no information.

Now, if we use the contribution margin approach and want to know what the impact on profits will be with a 10 percent increase, we can see that they will increase by *about* $450. Sales and the variable costs will increase by *something close to* 10 percent while fixed costs remain constant. Note that we said "something close to" 10 percent. Revenues and variable costs will not be exactly proportional to changes in volume, but they will generally be quite close. We are dealing here with future estimates and, unless we know otherwise, about as close to reality as we can get is to assume revenues and variable costs will vary proportionately with changes in volume. It is a realistic assumption.

The contribution margin approach is useful because it allows us to estimate what the impact on profits might be for a host of different operating, production and marketing decisions. The cost-volume-profit model is built on the basic accounting equation (Total Revenues − Total Costs = Profit) and some very simple math.

Some Basic Math

To determine the breakeven sales quantity for a firm or a project, divide fixed costs by the contribution margin per unit. For those who like mathematical formulas, we can illustrate. At its breakeven point a firm's total revenues and total costs are equal. We can express this as TR = TC. Knowing that total costs contain both fixed and variable costs, we can rewrite this equation as TR = TFC + TVC.

Since total revenue is equal to price times quantity and total variable costs are equal to variable cost per unit times quantity, we can further disaggregate our equation to

$$P \times Q = TFC + (VC_{per\ unit} \times Q)$$

That is, at breakeven, total revenue (price times quantity) equals total costs [total fixed costs plus (variable cost per unit times quantity)].

Continuing with our math tutorial, to solve for that quantity where a project will break even, we need to get all the expressions containing Q on the same side of the equation. Our equation then becomes:

$$(P \times Q) - (VC_{pu} \times Q) = TFC$$

After factoring Q, this can be written as

$$Q\,(P - VC_{pu}) = TFC$$

Therefore,

$$\text{breakeven } Q = \frac{TFC}{P - VC_{pu}}$$

In plain English, to solve for a project's breakeven quantity, divide its total fixed costs by its contribution margin per unit.

To summarize, algebraically, at breakeven quantity, TR = TC

or TR = TFC + TVC

or $P \times Q = TFC + (VC_{per\ unit} \times Q)$

or $(P \times Q) - (VC_{pu} \times Q) = TFC$

or $Q\,(P - VC_{pu}) = TFC$

or $Q = \dfrac{TFC}{P - VC_{pu}}$

Let's play around with this formula, see how it works and expand on it.

Cost-Volume-Profit Analysis Illustrated

Vino Vintners is thinking about introducing a new line of wine-in-a-box. It estimates that fixed costs will be $20,000 a year, variable costs of producing the wine and packaging it will be $2.00 per liter, and it will be able to sell the wine for $3.50 per liter. How many boxes of wine must it sell to break even? The answer is $20,000 ÷ ($3.50 − $2.00) = 13,333 boxes. Vinny Vito, the head vintner, is not interested in just breaking even. He says it will require an initial investment of $50,000 to get this project up and running and he needs at least a 10 percent return on his investment. That is, he needs to make an annual profit of at least $5,000. How many boxes does Vinny need to make a profit of $5,000? If we add the required profit to his total fixed costs and divide by the contribution margin per unit, we get ($20,000 + $5,000) ÷ $1.50; we find he needs to sell 16,667 boxes.

There is just one slight problem with that answer. The problem is taxes. That $5,000 profit is pre-tax. When we calculated breakeven quantity we didn't have to worry about taxes, but if we are trying to calculate required sales quantity for a target profit we need to take taxes into account. Let's assume Vito faces a tax rate of 35 percent. How much before-tax profit must he earn to have $5,000 after tax?

If we divide our required after-tax profit by one minus the tax rate $(1 - TR)$, the result will be our required before-tax profit. In Vinny's case, that answer is $5,000 ÷ 0.65 = $7,692. A before-tax profit of $7,692 will yield an after-tax income of $5,000 if the tax rate is 35 percent.

Now, how many boxes of wine does Vinny need to sell in order to earn $5,000 after-tax and make his investment worthwhile? The answer is ($20,000 + $7,692) ÷ $1.50 = 18,461 boxes. Now that we have the basic C-V-P model, let's see how Vinny can use it.

The first thing Vinny might want to do is perform a market study to see if there is an annual market for 18,461 boxes of wine. If there isn't, he can pass on this opportunity and save his $50,000 investment.

For our purposes, however, let's assume Vinny discovers there is a strong market for wine-in-a-box, and he estimates he can sell 30,000 boxes a year. At 30,000 boxes, how much will his annual after-tax income and the return on his investment be? He knows that he has a contribution margin of $1.50 per box, so his total contribution margin will be 30,000 × $1.50 = $45,000. With fixed costs of $20,000, his before-tax profit will be $45,000 − $20,000 = $25,000, leaving him with $25,000 × 0.65 = $16,250 after tax. This amounts to a return on his initial investment of $16,250 ÷ $50,000 = 32.5%. Not bad; looks like wine-in-a-box is a winner. Vinny now starts thinking of different ways he can use this powerful tool to manage his company.

He starts by doing additional marketing surveys. He believes that, if he reduces the price from $3.50 to $3.10 per liter, he can increase sales from 30,000 to 36,000 boxes a year. What will his after-tax profits be if he chooses to lower his prices? His contribution margin per unit decreases to $1.10, so his total contribution margin will become 36,000 × $1.10 = $39,600, his before-tax profit will be $39,600 − $20,000 = $19,600 and his after-tax profits fall to $19,600 × 0.65 = $12,740. Clearly this is not a good idea for Vinny. He could, however, use this same type of analysis to see what the results would be if he went upscale and charged $4.00 per liter.

In addition to marketing decisions, Vinny can also use C-V-P analysis for investment and operating decisions. Vinny discovers that he can buy automated production equipment which will increase his fixed costs by $10,000 per year, but reduce his variable costs by 20 percent. Should he undertake this option? If he does, his fixed costs become $30,000 per year, his variable costs will be $1.60 and his contribution margin will become $1.90. His new breakeven point will be higher, $30,000 ÷ $1.90 = 15,789 boxes (versus 13,333 boxes before automating). This doesn't look encouraging, but what will his profits look like at the expected sales level of 30,000 boxes? His expected before-tax profits if he automates will become (30,000 × $1.90) − $30,000 = $27,000. This translates into after-tax profits of $27,000 × 0.65 = $17,550, which is greater than his earlier profits of $16,250.

How can it be that Vinny will increase his profits at 30,000 boxes and yet increase his breakeven point from 13,333 boxes to 15,789?

It's because he has increased the firm's operating leverage. He has taken on greater fixed costs while reducing his variable costs per unit. This action increases his risks (he must now sell more to cover his fixed costs), but increases his potential for higher profits.

Herein lies one of the great managerial benefits of C-V-P analysis. It permits this type of "what-if" analysis. Once we have identified our fixed and variable costs and our revenues we can play around with the numbers and see what effect different strategies will have on profits. More formal presentations may refer to this as sensitivity analysis. It is a way to see how sensitive the dependent variables (contribution margins and profits) are to changes in the independent variables (variable and fixed costs and volume). Whatever it's called, there is great value in being able to estimate the result of a strategy before taking the leap and investing a lot of money.

This type of analysis worked great for Vinny and will work well for anyone trying to make a decision about a single product. But decisions often revolve around many products. Think about Wal-Mart or your local supermarket. Don't you suppose the executives who decide whether to open a new store have a pretty good idea that the store will be profitable before investing the millions of dollars necessary to get it up and running? But clearly it would be impossible to sit down and calculate the breakeven point for all the different products they offer and then try to predict how many of each item they will sell.

To perform C-V-P analysis involving multiple products we need to know what our total fixed costs are and what our variable costs are as a percentage of total revenues. There are a number of statistical techniques such as regression analysis that can be used to give us this information. One quite simple technique that can be used is known as the high–low method. The high–low method is predicated on the notion that the change in total costs which accompanies a change in volume is due to the change in total variable costs. That is, as volume increases, fixed costs remain constant and the increase in total costs is due entirely to increases in total variable costs. We can express this mathematically as: change in volume × variable cost per unit = change in total costs.

Butterfield Stores is a regional supermarket chain in the Midwest. They currently have six stores and are considering opening a seventh store in the Kansas City area. Obviously they are not going to open the store unless they feel they can return a reasonable profit. The estimated cost of acquiring land, building the store and stocking it with inventory is $5 million. Butterfield Stores' cost of capital is 8 percent, meaning the store will need to provide an annual after-tax profit of $400,000. Recent data from a store comparable to the one contemplated is:

Month	Sales	Total Costs
January	$800,000	$750,000
February	750,000	730,000
March	735,000	740,000
April	780,000	750,000
May	790,000	745,000
June	700,000	670,000
July	680,000	665,000
August	650,000	642,000
September	725,000	700,000
October	760,000	732,000
November	810,000	755,000
December	815,000	760,000

The next step is to compare the high-volume period sales and costs with the low-volume period. In this case the high-volume month is December, and the low-volume month is August.

Month	Sales	Total Costs
December	$815,000	$760,000
August	650,000	642,000
Difference	$165,000	$118,000

For Butterfield Stores, sales varied by $165,000 and total costs varied by $118,000. If we assume that fixed costs are truly fixed, the change in total costs is due to changes in variable costs and that variable costs are 71.5 percent of sales ($118,000 ÷ $165,000). If variable costs are 71.5 percent of sales, then Butterfield Stores' contribution margin is 28.5 percent of sales (100 − 71.5). How much then are Butterfield Stores' fixed costs? In December their variable costs were $815,000 × 0.715 = $582,725. Fixed costs would then be $760,000 − $582,850 = $177,275.

Let's compare this with August's numbers. Total variable costs are $650,000 × 0.715 = $464,750 and fixed costs would be $642,000 − $464,750 = $177,250. The $25 difference in fixed costs between December and August is merely due to rounding. We now have the information we need to perform C-V-P analysis for Butterfield Stores.

We cannot determine how many units they must sell to break even, simply because different items provide different contribution margins. We can, however, determine the total dollar sales they must have to break even or earn any given profit. The formula is:

$$\text{Breakeven Sales Dollars} = \frac{\text{Total Fixed Costs}}{\text{Contribution Margin Ratio}}$$

The contribution margin ratio is the ratio of a firm's contribution margin to its sales (Contribution Margin ÷ Sales). Butterfield Stores' breakeven sales dollar amount is $177,275 ÷ 0.285 = $622,018.

Remember we earlier said Butterfield Stores were thinking of opening another store in the Kansas City area. If the cost to do so is $5 million, their cost of capital is 8 percent and their tax rate is 35 percent, how much does the store need to sell in order to make the investment profitable? Our formula becomes

$$\text{Required Sales} = \frac{\text{Total Fixed Costs} + (\text{Desired After-Tax Profit}/1 - \text{Tax Rate})}{\text{Contribution Margin Ratio}}$$

Butterfield Stores will need an after-tax profit of $400,000 ($5,000,000 × .08). The calculation of required sales is [$177,275 + ($400,000/0.65)] ÷ 0.285 = $2,781,260. Armed with this information

Butterfield Stores' managers are now in a position to do market research and determine if they can sustain this level of sales. This is the type of analysis that Wal-Mart, Target, Sears and grocery chains perform whenever they consider expanding.

What we have just described for both Vino Vintners and Butterfield Stores is a model of their operations. The validity of any model depends on how near to the real-world phenomenon it actually is. Think of yourself as a test pilot for Boeing. You are preparing to take their latest model jet fighter up to 30,000 feet. This plane has never been flown that high before. Somebody has to be the first one to fly it, and your name was drawn out of the hat. As you are being strapped into the pilot's seat you may be praying that the computer models they used in designing this plane were based on solid, real-world data. If they weren't, your flight might be less than successful. Using a C-V-P model to make operating and marketing decisions may not quicken your pulse quite as much as our test pilot's, but the point is made. If you are to be successful, your model must reflect reality.

The nice thing about modeling a firm's operations is that you can manipulate the model before trying out the real thing. For example, you can estimate what will happen to profits if you automate and increase fixed costs but lower variable cost per unit or what the result will be if you change the sales mix and sell more widgets, but less gidgets. What will the result be if you increase price 10 percent, but volume decreases 12 percent? Understanding of these relationships and factoring them into our model make intelligent analysis possible, leading to better planning, control and decision making.

Assumptions

The C-V-P model we have described makes four important assumptions. While not strictly correlating with reality in most situations, they probably come close enough to allow us to have a very good idea of the consequences of our decision. These assumptions are:

1   Revenues change proportionately with volume. That is, if we sell 10 percent more units our revenues will increase 10

percent. This assumption holds true as long as we do not have to lower prices in order to increase sales.

2   Total variable costs change proportionately with volume. This assumption holds true as long as our variable costs per unit do not change.

3   We know what our fixed costs are and they will remain fixed over any anticipated change in output.

4   Inventory levels remain constant.

It may be good to reiterate that, when we make decisions about new products, new markets, new production techniques and so on, we are dealing with estimates and projections, not necessarily exact and complete data. We never really know how precise our estimates and forecasts are. How far off can we be and still make a good decision? To answer that, we must understand C-V-P relationships and do sensitivity analysis.

Sensitivity Analysis

Sensitivity ('what-if') analysis allows us to examine how an outcome might change if our predictions about costs or volume do not pan out. We can use sensitivity analysis to determine such things as how much our sales need to be in order to earn a desired profit. We can also use it when making decisions such as whether to spend money on an advertising campaign, whether to lower or raise prices, or whether to automate and incur fixed expenses in order to reduce variable expenses. The following exercise illustrates these points.

Partner's Produce is a West-Coast chain of grocery outlets. Given the unsettled state of the economy and possibly adverse agricultural conditions they are unsure of what the coming year holds for them. They have, however, put together the following tentative budget:

Revenues	$15,000,000
Fixed costs	3,000,000
Variable costs	10,000,000

1   What is Partner's Produce contribution margin?
2   What is Partner's Produce contribution margin ratio?
3   What are Partner's Produce breakeven sales?
4   What will their profit be if sales volume increases/decreases by
    10 percent?
5   What will their breakeven sales be if their fixed costs increase/
    decrease by 6 percent?
6   What will the impact be on profits if we increase fixed costs by
    10 percent and decrease variable costs by 5 percent?

The answers to this problem are at the end of the chapter on
page 54.

Operating Leverage

Operating leverage is closely related to the concepts we have been
discussing. Operating leverage is the extent to which a firm's operations involve fixed costs. The greater the fixed costs vis-à-vis variable
costs, the more highly leveraged a firm is. Being highly leveraged
means that a relatively small change in sales results in a large change
in operating income. During a good year, a high degree of leverage works to increase income relative to what it would otherwise be.
During a bad year, it works to decrease income (or increase losses).
Leverage is a two-edged sword. Higher leverage means higher risks
and higher profit or loss potential. We can illustrate this concept with
the following example. Both companies sell the same product and
compete in the same market.

	Company A	Company B
Sales price	$10	$10
Variable cost/unit	6	4
Fixed costs	$80,000	$140,000
Unit sales	30,000	30,000

Their respective income statements are:

	Company A	Company B
Sales (30,000 units)	$300,000	$300,000
Variable costs	180,000	120,000
Contribution margin	120,000	180,000
Fixed costs	80,000	140,000
Operating profit	$40,000	$40,000

Selling the same product in the same market and making the same profit, these two firms look quite similar. At second glance, however, we can tell that Company B is the more highly leveraged of the two, as its fixed costs are greater as compared to its variable costs. What will happen if they both enjoy a 10 percent increase in units sold? Their respective income statements will be:

	Company A	Company B
Sales (33,000 units)	$330,000	$330,000
Variable costs	198,000	132,000
Contribution margin	132,000	198,000
Fixed costs	80,000	140,000
Operating profit	$52,000	$58,000

Clearly, Company B, because of its greater leverage, came out ahead. What happens, however, when a recession comes along or competitors come into the market and take away some of the market share? Do the math and you will find that, if each company's sales decreased by 10 percent from the original, Company A would have operating profits of $28,000 while Company B would have operating profits of only $22,000. So, is it better to be more or less leveraged? It depends on your attitude toward risk. How optimistic or pessimistic are you?

Summary

This chapter addresses: (1) cost-volume-profit analysis; (2) sensitivity analysis for different marketing and operating decisions; and (3) the impact of operating leverage on a firm's operating profit.

Concepts were introduced in Chapter 2 to illustrate how variable, fixed and mixed costs and a firm's volume of sales impact its operating income. Using different cost-volume-profit models this chapter introduces the concept of contribution margin and develops a contribution margin based income statement. It illustrates how the contribution margin approach is superior to the so-called traditional income statement for purposes of management planning, control and decision making.

Understanding cost-volume-profit relationships is crucial for performing sensitivity (or "what-if") analysis. Such analysis allows one to predict what the result will be of changes in the firm's cost structure as well as changes in the volume of output. This understanding is vital for planning and decision making.

This chapter also discussed the notion of operating leverage. Operating leverage is the amount of fixed costs a firm employs in comparison to its variable costs. The greater the proportion of fixed costs, the higher the degree of operating leverage. Operating leverage is a two-edged sword. In a highly leveraged firm, profits will increase or decrease at a higher rate of change than sales volume. In a highly leveraged firm, when times are good they are very, very good; when they are bad they are horrid.

Answer to Partner's Produce Problem

1   $5,000,000
2   33.3%
3   $9,009,009 (rounded)
4   10% increase: $2,500,000; 10% decrease: $1,500,000
5   6% increase: $9,549,350 (rounded); 6% decrease: $8,468,468 (rounded)
6   New breakeven sales: $8,991,826; new profit: $2,200,000

Exercises

1   Olivia Blueberry, owner of Blueberry Bicycles, is considering an offer to operate a booth at the Metro Bike show this coming weekend. The promoters of the bike show have offered Olivia

two options: (1) a fixed payment of $3,000 for the weekend; or (2) 10 percent of total sales during the show. Blueberry Bicycles sell for $1,000 and cost Olivia $700.

(a) What is the breakeven point in dollar sales for each option?
(b) At what level of sales will Olivia be indifferent to the two options?
(c) Which option will Olivia prefer if sales are expected to be in excess of your answer to (b)?

2 Denali Skateboards manufactures and sells several different skateboard models. Denali produces skateboards in batches and currently produces ten batches per year. He faces a tax rate of 35 percent.

Using the following information determine how many skateboards Denali must sell in order to (a) break even, (b) earn an after-tax profit of $18,000.

Average skateboard sales price	$125.00
Direct materials per unit	$15.00
Direct labor per unit	$20.00
Test and inspection per unit	$1.50
Packaging per unit	$4.00
Sales commission per unit	$7.50
Rent per month	$1,000
Insurance per year	$3,000
Utilities per year (average)	$4,000

3 House of the Sun Foods produce packaged gourmet vegan dinners. The selling price per dinner is $30. The variable cost per dinner is $18 and their fixed costs per month are $5,000. Last month they sold 500 dinners. In anticipation of the coming holidays, they plan on increasing sales 20 percent. Their tax rate is 20 percent.

(a) Calculate House of the Sun Foods' contribution margin per dinner.
(b) Calculate their breakeven quantity per month.
(c) What was their after-tax profit or loss last month?
(d) What is their anticipated after-tax profit or loss for next month?
(e) How many meals do they need to sell in order to earn an after-tax profit of $2,000 per month?

4   Two furniture manufacturers have the following cost structures.

	Ye Olde Furniture	Ye Newe Furniture
Sales	$1,000,000	$1,000,000
Variable costs	700,000	500,000
Fixed costs	200,000	400,000
Operating income	$100,000	$100,000

What will their respective operating incomes be if their sales volumes increase 10 percent? Decrease 10 percent? Explain the difference.

4

DECISION MAKING I:
THE BASICS

Chapter Overview

This chapter presents a model for decision making and discusses the role and uses of data in decision making. After studying this chapter you will:

- Understand the difference between quantitative and qualitative information;
- Be able to recognize information that is relevant to a decision;
- Understand the components of a basic decision model;
- Understand the role of incremental data in decision making.

* * * * *

Decision making involves identifying and choosing between two or more alternatives. You cannot consistently make good decisions without relevant, reliable information, and the single most important role of any accounting system is to provide that information. Good judgment and relevant, reliable information lead to good decisions.

Information can be either quantitative or qualitative. Quantitative information is that to which you can attach numbers; qualitative deals with non-numerical attributes or traits. Quantitative information is more objective: we can all agree that ten dollars is more than three. Qualitative information refers to an object's characteristics and tends to be more subjective with respect to the decision maker. Is a Honda of higher quality than a Toyota or a Ford? What is the basis of your comparison? Performance? Safety? Appearance, etc.? Is a rose as pretty as a daisy?

Furthermore, different qualitative factors are important to different decision makers. If you are deciding whether to buy a house or rent an apartment, perhaps location and the proximity of neighbors are important. For someone else, these factors may play a secondary role to freedom from maintenance and ease of moving.

Basic Decision Model

Business decisions are never made in a vacuum. Constraints are inevitable. You have to make decisions now. You're never sure you have enough information to make the best decision. If only you had time to gather and analyze more data. Also, you're constrained by a budget. If you had more money to work with, you could have more options, which would lead to better results. If only you had more time you could run more tests, and on and on.

Think about a major decision you made recently. Maybe it was to buy a car, move out of state to take a job, get married, or something similar. Now think about the process you used. If you went through a process similar to the following, you increased your chances of making a good decision.

Perhaps you began by gathering both quantitative and qualitative information. Since this was a major decision, you did not make it impulsively. Nor did you rely on just one source of information but sought out unbiased opinions from dependable sources. You knew from past experience that without good, reliable, relevant information you were likely to rue the outcome.

After you gathered the information you needed, you probably made some sort of prediction. That is, you tried to imagine what the future might be like if you made one particular decision versus a different one.

With the information in hand and a notion about what the future implications of the various alternatives might be, you finally chose an alternative and you implemented it. You bought the car, you decided to not take the job, you held off on getting married (or not).

Ever since you made your decision you may have been second-guessing yourself. That is to say, you have been re-evaluating both your decision and your decision-making skills. That's a normal reaction and is a good thing to do. Few decisions are so obvious and so cut and dried that they don't deserve some after-the-fact review.

It would be nice if following the above steps could guarantee a good outcome. It won't, of course, but it will increase the likelihood of making better decisions.

Managers are continuously making decisions that range from the humdrum and largely inconsequential to the strategic which may well decide the future of their organization and the welfare of employees, suppliers and customers. They need reliable and relevant information in order to make good decisions.

This, of course, begs the question. What is it that makes information both reliable and relevant? The Financial Accounting Standards Board addressed this question in *Statement of Financial Accounting Concepts No. 2, Qualitative Characteristics of Accounting Information* (1980). They posited that, to be both reliable and relevant, information must be timely and predictive, offer feedback and be verifiable and unbiased. In addition, to be relevant to any given decision, information must vary among alternatives. Let's explore these concepts.

Reliable and Relevant Information

Predictive. Relevant information consists of expected future data, not historical data. Since decisions have an impact on the future, relevant information should inform us of the likely future consequences of our decisions. If we spend a million dollars to increase fuel efficiency we want to know how much we will save on utility costs.

Feedback. Information should provide us with feedback on how we are doing. Immediate feedback is better than delayed feedback. A great example of a system that provides us with instant feedback is the speedometer in our cars. It tells us how fast we are going at the present time. In fact, it's a far better system than the flashing red lights in the rearview mirror.

Timely. Timely information shows itself in "good time," that is, its occurrence is opportune, suitable to the moment or to a particular time, and adapted to the occasion. Information that is not timely is merely historical. Historical information is just that: it's about what did happen. Historical costs are sunk costs. As we said earlier, no matter what we do, we're not going to get them back. Historical data *per se* is irrelevant for decision making. That last sentence should raise some eyebrows. After all, don't we rely on history for guidance when making decisions? Yes. Haven't we all heard the old cliché, "Those who ignore history are bound to repeat it?" Yes. Furthermore, aren't a firm's balance sheet and income statements based on historical data? Yes. Does this mean that financial statements are of no use for decision making? No.

There is continuity between the past, the present and the future. The value of historical data is that we can use the relationships it reveals to make informed forecasts. Analysis of a firm's financial statements reveals those relationships. If the firm's cost of goods sold has consistently been 60 percent of sales over the past several years, there's a good chance it will also be close to 60 percent of sales next year unless something significantly different happens. If overhead has consistently been 125 percent of direct labor for the past several years it will in all probability continue to be so. Consequently, we can generally rely on historical data to aid us in making reasoned estimates about the future.

Verifiable. Verification provides a degree of assurance that accounting measures really do represent what they say they represent. For accounting information to be verifiable, different observers looking at the same data should get the same measure. When a company gets a "clean" audit report, it's because independent auditors have examined the firm's records and financial statements and have confirmed that the financial statements "present fairly in all material respects" the financial position of the firm. In other words, competent evidence substantiates assets and liabilities and that income figures have been verified.

Non-biased information is free from opinion or preconceptions. Its neutrality does not attempt to promote any particular agenda. For an example of information that is not neutral, think of information provided by the "other" political party.

Varies among alternatives. If a piece of information is the same for different alternatives, it's irrelevant. If we plan to buy machine A or machine B and if we are going to hire an operator at a salary of $50,000 per year regardless of which machine we buy, the operator's salary is not relevant. On the other hand, if one machine is more energy efficient than the other, our expected future utility bills are very relevant.

* * * * *

If we include any information other than "expected future information that varies amongst alternatives" in our decision model, the very best we can hope for is that the information does not have an impact. If it does, the outcome will be less than optimal. Always.

Good decision making relies on incremental analysis. Incremental analysis is simply the process of looking at the *different* results of one decision versus those of another. From a management perspective it means looking at the differences between such things as revenues, costs, profits or cash flows from pursuing one course of action versus another.

Egg McMuffins provide an excellent example of where a firm made a decision using incremental analysis. It is now common for fast food restaurants to open early and provide some type of breakfast sandwich along with coffee, juice and pastries. It wasn't that terribly long ago, however, that these restaurants did not open until 11 a.m., just in time for the lunch trade. After a market study McDonald's management came to the conclusion that the incremental cost of opening earlier was far smaller than the incremental contribution to be made from serving breakfasts, and the egg was hatched, so to speak.

Opportunity Costs

Opportunity costs represent income lost from forgone opportunities. Opportunity costs relate to transactions that do not occur. Consequently no accounting record is made and they are often overlooked. A good example of an opportunity cost is the cost of going to college. Let's suppose that tuition, books and supplies cost $20,000 per year. (Ignore room and board. You have to live and eat somewhere.) What is the total cost of going to college? It depends on your alternatives. If you are 18 years old with no particular skills, perhaps the best you can do is flip burgers at $8.50 an hour. If you work full time for a year you would earn about $17,000. The total cost of going to college would then be $37,000. If you could find work paying $20.00 an hour, your cost of going to college would be significantly higher. In deciding to go to college, you have to balance that, of course, with the cost of not going to college, and don't forget qualitative as well as quantitative considerations. (As an aside, what would have been the opportunity cost to LeBron James of spending four years in college?)

Examples

Managers often make mistakes by including fixed costs and sunk costs when making decisions. Here are two examples.

For the first example, suppose you're considering the purchase of a new computer. You have two alternatives: to buy or not to buy. The computer system you're thinking about buying will cost $100,000, but it will let you reduce operating costs by $50,000 a year for four years before it needs to be replaced. It will replace a computer system that you bought ten years ago, is fully depreciated and runs software that is out of date. Should you buy? Yes, this is a good deal. It will save you $200,000 over four years; this represents a 35 percent return on investment. You would definitely want to buy the new machine under these circumstances.

In the second example, the facts about the new computer are the same as in the first example. That is, you will save $50,000 a year for four years. This time however the new computer system would replace one you bought just last month for $125,000. If you buy the new computer you will now have invested $225,000 in computers over the past month. To make matters worse, let's also assume you will have to scrap the one you just recently bought. Now it's not such a good deal to buy the new computer, right? Wrong. It's still a good deal. It still represents a return on investment of 35 percent.

It doesn't matter when you bought the old computer or how much you paid for it. Those costs are sunk and irrelevant to the replacement decision. They're history, and nothing you can do will alter that fact. The expected future data for our decision are a cost of $100,000 and savings of $200,000 over four years. That still represents an annual rate of return of 35 percent. Unless your other investments are earning more than 35 percent, you should buy the new computer. It's a good deal, period.

There is a time value of money concerning the difference between writing off the $125,000 when we scrap the current computer versus taking depreciation on it over its life. The difference, however, is small and would not be enough to influence our decision in this case. We'll discuss the time value of money and its impact on decision making in Chapter 5.

Many costs that are relevant for decision making in the long run may be irrelevant in the short run. This is because some will be fixed in the short run but variable over a longer period of time. Examples include such costs as depreciation, contracted salaries, monthly rent and insurance expense.

The basic difference between the short run and the long run is whether or not a firm's capacity can be changed. In the short run, capacity is fixed. In the long run, it can be increased. These are relative notions. What might be the long run for one firm might well be the short run for another.

Consider the following example: One firm makes men's neckties; the other produces steel. How long would it take to increase the output of the necktie manufacturer? For starters, the firm would have to hire some workers, train them in the art of tie-making, and lease some sewing machines and a place to do the work. How long would that take? Maybe a month, maybe two? Now consider the steel producer. How long will it take to build a new steel-producing facility and hire and train a workforce? It could likely take a couple of years, if not longer.

For the tie producer in our example, three months is the long run.

For the steel producer, 18 months is the short run. Understanding the distinction between the short and long run is important for decision making because a cost that is fixed and irrelevant in the short run may very well be incremental and very relevant in the long run.

One of the hidden dangers in using cost data for decision making is allocated fixed costs. If we report that the unit cost of a widget is $25, a manager might proceed on the assumption that, if he produces ten more units, total costs will increase by $250. This, however, will most likely not be the case. That $25 unit cost is made up of labor, materials and overhead. Overhead generally consists of both variable and fixed costs. While the cost of labor and materials can usually be traced directly to the product, overhead cannot. We might know that the material that goes into a widget cost $5 and that it took $10 of labor, but how much insurance, rent and depreciation are in the cost of a widget? The amount of these overhead items in the $25 is solely due to the fact that we decided, arbitrarily, to allocate that amount of fixed overhead costs to widgets and not to different products we manufacture.

The fixed overhead costs are not going to change with the decision to produce or not produce more widgets. If we include the full cost of the widgets in our decision model we will be including irrelevant data and heading toward a poor decision.

Here are two examples of decisions managers might face. Note how including irrelevant information in a decision model will lead to a poor decision.

In the first example, the Parker Corporation manufactures and installs lighting fixtures. The company estimates the cost of making and installing fixtures for St. Mary's Hospital to be as follows:

Materials	$50,000
Direct manufacturing labor	10,000
Direct installation labor	12,000
Variable overhead (allocated on manufacturing labor)	44,000
Fixed overhead (allocated on manufacturing labor)	150,000
Total costs	$266,000

St. Mary's and Parker Corporation agreed on a price of $325,000 for the job. Owing to circumstances beyond its control, Parker finds itself eight days behind schedule. The contract with St. Mary's stipulated a fine of $2,500 per day if the project is finished beyond the scheduled date. William Parker, the owner of Parker Corporation, is considering ordering pre-made fixture components at a cost of $35,000. If he uses the pre-made components, total materials costs will increase by $20,000 and direct manufacturing labor will decrease by $3,000. This course of action will allow him to reduce the time over schedule from eight days to five and reduce the penalty from $20,000 to $12,500.

Should Parker Corporation purchase the pre-made components? To answer the question, we need to consider which data is relevant, that is, which data varies amongst the alternatives (to buy or not to buy).

Materials cost is relevant. These costs will increase from $50,000 to $70,000. Direct manufacturing labor is relevant. These costs will decrease from $10,000 to $7,000. Direct installation labor is not relevant. The fixtures will have to be installed regardless of who makes them or how they are made. Variable overhead is relevant only if it truly varies with direct labor. Fixed overhead is not relevant. Even though Parker Corporation allocates it on the basis of direct labor costs, it is still a fixed cost and will not vary with our decision. The cost of the penalty is obviously relevant.

The conclusion, based on our analysis to date, is that Parker Corporation should not buy the pre-made fixtures.

	Buy	Do Not Buy
Cost of materials	$70,000	$50,000
Cost of direct manufacturing labor	7,000	10,000
Cost of direct installation labor	N/A	N/A
Variable overhead	7,000	10,000
Cost of fixed overhead	N/A	N/A
Penalty	12,500	20,000
Total relevant costs	96,500	$90,000

If the Parker Corporation had allocated fixed overhead costs, which do not change, on the basis of the change in manufacturing labor, they would have gotten very different results: $150,000 would have been allocated to the Do Not Buy alternative and $105,000 to the Buy alternative. If they had relied on this outcome they would have made a poor decision.

Here's another example. Blueberry Bicycles manufactures and sells three lines of bicycles (mountain bikes, racing bikes and hybrids). The firm's accountant has prepared the following report. Fixed costs have been allocated on the basis of number of units sold.

	Mountain	Racing	Hybrid	Total
Units	500	300	900	1,700
Sales	$300,000	$400,000	$600,000	$1,300,000
Less variable costs:				
Materials	90,000	120,000	210,000	420,000
Labor	80,000	105,000	180,000	365,000
Overhead	60,000	90,000	150,000	300,000
Contribution margin	70,000	85,000	60,000	215,000
Fixed costs (lease, depreciation, etc.)	45,000	27,000	81,000	153,000
Profit/(loss)	$25,000	$58,000	$(21,000)	$62,000

The president of Blueberry Bikes looked at this analysis and said, "Clearly, the hybrid line is a loser and we should close it down. After all, it lost $21,000 last year." Is she right? Let's look a bit more closely. After dropping the line of hybrid bikes Blueberry's income statement will look like this:

	Mountain	Racing	Total
Units	500	300	800
Sales	$300,000	$400,000	$700,000

Less variable costs			
Materials	90,000	120,000	210,000
Labor	80,000	105,000	185,000
Overhead	60,000	90,000	150,000
Contribution margin	70,000	85,000	155,000
Fixed costs (lease, depreciation, etc.)	95,625	57,375	153,000
Profit (Loss)	$(25,625)	$27,625	$2,000

If we close down the hybrid line we will now have only the mountain and racing bikes over which we can spread the fixed costs of $153,000. If sales of the remaining two product lines remain constant and we continue to allocate fixed costs on the basis of units sold, we will now allocate $95,625 to mountain bikes and $57,375 to racing bikes. This results in a so-called profit of $27,625 for racing bikes and a loss of $25,625 for mountain bikes. What happens if we now drop mountain bikes?

The president should not have included fixed costs in her analysis. These costs will be incurred regardless of her decision. Once again, the only relevant costs are those which vary with the decision.

The thing to note about this last example is that hybrid bikes were making a positive contribution of $60,000. They showed a "loss" in the accountant's report only because $81,000 of fixed overhead had been allocated to them. A different, equally defensible, allocation method would have resulted in different profits and losses being reported for each of the three product lines. The moral of the story for managers is: Know your costs. Know how they behave. Know what causes them.

So far in this chapter we have emphasized the importance of quantitative information in decision making. The qualitative aspects of decision making are no less important and in many cases take precedence. For most of us, the most important life decision we make – whom to marry or not marry – is made largely on the basis of qualitative considerations. (Then again, some of us look closely at our partner-to-be's balance sheet before committing.)

Let's go back and consider the qualitative considerations in Parker Corporation's decision to make the fixtures and incur the penalty for late completion. Aside from saving $6,000, if they make the fixtures themselves they now have complete control over the quality of the fixtures. Their reputation for quality fixtures may be of utmost importance to them. They will also more fully utilize their workforce, which in turn can lead to higher employee morale. On the other hand, they will have to pay a penalty and in addition to the fine (quantitative data) they may gain a reputation as a firm that cannot bring a job in on time. These are all qualitative factors to be considered.

Summary

This chapter looks at some of the decisions managers make on a routine basis and the role accounting plays in providing the information they need to make these decisions. For information to be relevant it must be predictive, offer feedback, be timely and vary among the alternatives facing the decision maker. To be reliable, information must be verifiable and non-biased. This chapter emphasizes the fact that, if irrelevant information is included in a decision model and if it influences a decision, the decision will always be less than optimal.

This chapter discusses the factors that make up a basic decision model and the difference between quantitative and qualitative information. It emphasized the importance of incremental data, that is, the data which varies among alternative decisions.

To illustrate the use of accounting data for decision making, this chapter looks at decisions such as whether to make or buy components; whether to accept or reject special offers to sell goods and services at below current sales prices; and whether to drop or keep poorly performing product lines and divisions.

Exercises

1   Define the following terms:
    (a) Relevant information
    (b) Incremental analysis

(c) Sunk costs
(d) Opportunity costs
(e) Allocation
(f) Differential cost

2   List two possible qualitative advantages of making rather than
     buying a component.
3   DBL, Inc. normally operates at approximately 90 percent of capac-
     ity. Owing to a temporary downturn in the economy it is presently
     operating at 70 percent of capacity. It currently produces 35,000
     units of patented bearings designed for use in heating and cooling
     systems. Its accountant prepared the following cost schedule:

Raw materials	$14.00 per unit
Direct labor	$6.00 per unit
Variable overhead	$5.00 per unit
Fixed overhead	$225,000 per year (operating at 90% capacity this comes to $5.00 per unit, at 70% capacity fixed overhead per unit is $6.43)

The normal selling price is $40.00 per unit. An Australian company
has approached DBL, Inc. about purchasing 10,000 units. The sale
would be a one-time-only sale and would not impact their other business. The Australian company has offered to pay $28 per unit.

(a) What is DBL, Inc.'s cost per unit for the bearings at 90 percent
     capacity. At 70 percent?
(b) Should DBL, Inc. accept the offer? Why?
(c) What impact will this sale have on DBL, Inc.'s profit?
(d) What is the absolute lowest amount they should accept?
(e) What qualitative factors should DBL, Inc. consider?

4   Joe Skater owns an ice-skating rink that accommodates
     100 people. He charges $12 an hour to skate. Attendants receive
     $8 per hour to staff the entrance booth. Utilities, rent, deprecia-
     tion and insurance average $3,000 per month.

Recently the manager of an out-of-town hockey team approached Joe about renting the rink for a full day of practice on an upcoming Sunday for a lump sum of $1,300. If Joe accepts the offer, one attendant would be needed. Otherwise, two attendants will be needed. Normal operating hours on Sunday are from 11:00 a.m. to 6:00 p.m., and the average attendance is 16 skaters per hour.

Should Joe accept the hockey team's offer? By how much will Joe be better off by making the correct decision?

5

DECISION MAKING II: CAPITAL BUDGETING DECISIONS

Once a decision was made, I did not worry about it later.
(President Harry S. Truman)

Chapter Overview

This chapter discusses the time value of money and the principal capital budgeting decision models. After studying this chapter you will

- Realize the importance of making good capital investment decisions;
- Understand that, like all decisions, capital investment decisions should be based on incremental analysis;
- Understand why there is a time value to money;
- Understand how cash flows from a long-term investment are estimated;
- Be able to calculate the present value of these cash flows;
- Know how the net present value (NPV), internal rate of return (IRR), payback period and accounting rate of return (ARR) of a project are determined;
- Understand the limitations and dangers of using ARR to evaluate long-term investments.

In the previous chapter we talked about short-term decision making. In the short term, productive capacity is fixed and, as a consequence, so are certain costs. In this chapter we are going to expand our analysis by looking at decisions that have long-term implications and which frequently require large investments. These types of decisions often impact productive capacity and are generally referred to as either capital budgeting or capital expenditure decisions.

Short Term versus Long Term

Is it short term versus long term or short run versus long run? It's both. The literature uses these terms interchangeably, so we will too.

Many managerial accounting texts point out that in the short run many costs are fixed and in the long run few, if any, are fixed. This is true, but such a statement could lead one to the conclusion that there is only a short run and a long run and nothing in between. In reality, the budgeting process encompasses a continuum, as Figure 5.1 illustrates.

Capital Budgeting Decisions

Decisions relating to capital expenditures are not easily reversible. They generally involve large sums of money and long periods of time. So a poor decision of this sort is going to cost a lot of money and it is a decision you are going to have to live with for a long time. Not surprisingly, these are often thought to be among the most important decisions an organization can make.

More than one organization has declared bankruptcy solely because someone or some committee made a poor capital budgeting decision. Take a trip through your local industrial district and note the shuttered factories and warehouses. In how many cases had someone miscalculated their firm's future cash flows?

Really short run	Fairly short run	Mid-run	Fairly long run	Really long run
←————————————————————————————————————→				
All costs are fixed	Most costs are fixed	Some costs are fixed	Few costs are fixed	Hardly any costs are fixed

Figure 5.1

Short-term decisions relate more to day-to-day operations, while capital budgeting involves strategic decisions that affect long-term goals. Capital budgeting decisions may include decisions to buy or not to buy major pieces of equipment, to buy equipment from one manufacturer instead of another, to buy one machine versus a similar one, to introduce or not introduce a new product line, to expand overseas, to build a new plant and so on. Both short-term and long-term decisions should utilize incremental analysis.

In our discussion in the previous chapter we stressed that when making short-term decisions we want to rely only on relevant information. And we defined relevant information as "expected future information that varies amongst alternatives." The same approach and the same rules apply equally to long-term decisions. Both types of decisions should rely on a differential analysis of cash inflows and outflows.

The Time Value of Money

A significant difference in the two types of decisions is the time value of money, which does not need to be taken into account when making short-term decisions, but does so when making long-term, capital investment decisions. A dollar received today has greater value than a dollar to be received a year from now for three different reasons – risk, inflation and interest.

To illustrate, let's say I buy some merchandise from you on credit for a hundred dollars. If I'm a regular customer and tell you that I will put a check in the mail tomorrow (assuming I'm an honorable person and telling the truth) there is little risk that you will not be paid. If, however, I tell you I'll pay you in one year the risk goes up considerably. I might become bankrupt in the next 12 months, I might die or I might run off to Mexico.

If I tell you I'll pay you in two years, the risk level goes up even more. The longer the time between now and when you expect cash inflow from a project, the more the uncertainty and the greater the risk of not receiving the cash.

Another factor is inflation. Inflation erodes the purchasing power of money. If this coming year we have, say, 3 percent inflation, that means that the proverbial market basket of goods and services which costs $100 today will cost $103 this time next year. If I owe you $100 and don't pay for a year, it has cost you $3 in purchasing power. You want your money now.

Economists like to assume all manner of things to make their argument, so let's assume away risk and inflation for a moment. We'll assume that I'm completely reliable and there will be no inflation during the next 12 months. Let's further assume that you don't have an immediate need for the hundred dollars I owe you. Now, would you be indifferent to whether I paid you now or in a year?

No, you would not be indifferent. Even though I might be completely reliable and there will be no inflation, you still want your money now instead of later because of the institution of interest. If nothing else, you could take the money I owe you, buy a one-year certificate of deposit and earn some interest.

Estimating Future Cash Flows

Because there is a time value of money and because capital budgeting involves future cash inflows and outflows, we need to estimate how much those flows will be and when they will occur. We then want to use an appropriate interest rate to discount those cash flows to their present value.

The most difficult part of capital budgeting is estimating how much those future cash flows will be. It's important to understand that, as the life of a capital project increases, estimating future cash flows becomes more and more difficult. If the project's horizon is far enough in the future, many firms rely on little more than "scientific" guesses. It is helpful to consider cash flows from a project in four separate categories:

1   **Initial investment outflows.** These are mostly upfront cash flows and include such things as construction costs, the price of equipment, taxes, delivery, setup and training costs, plus the costs of initial inventory and additional funds for working capital involved in getting the equipment, plant or other project up and running. Of all the cash flows associated with a capital

project, these are the most immediate and are generally quite straightforward to estimate.

2   **Periodic operating cash flows.** These are positive cash flows which come from additional capacity and new products or from savings in labor, energy and other overhead costs. Estimating these cash flows for the first couple of years of a project is not particularly problematic, but, as we mentioned earlier, estimating later cash flows from operations becomes more and more difficult as the time horizon expands. Will that $40,000 savings in estimated labor costs for next year remain steady through all five years of a machine's life?

3   **Depreciation tax shield.** These are the cash flows associated with a capital project that can be most accurately forecast. They arise from tax savings due to depreciation and amortization of the project's costs. Recall from earlier discussions that depreciation and amortization are like any other expenses in that they reduce taxable income and hence tax expense. Unlike most other expenses, however, they are non-cash expenses. Assume we have a one-million-dollar capital project with an estimated ten-year life and that we have decided to fully depreciate it using the straight-line method. If annual depreciation related to the project is $100,000 and if the firm's tax rate is 40 percent, its annual tax bill will be lowered by $40,000 ($100,000 × 0.40). Reducing your tax bill by $40,000 is tantamount to a cash inflow of $40,000. If we do not change depreciation methods and tax rates do not change, we can very accurately forecast cash inflows from a project's depreciation tax shield.

4   **Disinvestment flows.** These cash flows come about when a capital project is finished, that is, when the equipment is retired, the plant shut down or the product line eliminated. Of the four different categories of cash flows, these are without a doubt the most difficult to forecast and their amount is usually little more than an educated guess.

When a capital project is finished there may be a cash inflow or outflow from the salvage of an asset. There may be a tax gain or

loss associated with its retirement. There may also be the return of
some working capital invested in the project. It's not hard to see that
estimating these amounts years before they occur involves a lot of
guesswork.

Present Value

Central to capital budgeting is finding the value today (i.e. the present
value) of future cash flows. Most financial calculators and Microsoft's
Excel program have a function that allows you to do these calculations. For those who like to do math in longhand, there are formulas.
There are also published present value tables (see Tables A and B in
the appendix to this chapter).

Let's have some fun and play around with these tables for a bit.
Table A shows the present value (the value today) of receiving one
dollar at some time in the future at different interest rates. It assumes
interest is compounded annually and that payment is made at the
end of each respective year. So, if we want to know what the value
today is of receiving $1 five years from now at 8 percent, we will go
down the left column to period 5 and trace over to the 8 percent column where we will find 0.681. This tells us that the present value of
receiving $1 in five years, if the interest rate is 8 percent, is $0.681. If
we want to know the value today of receiving $1,000 in five years at
8 percent we will merely multiply 0.681 times 1,000. The result will,
of course, be $681.

Here's another way of looking at this. If you put $681 in the bank
today at 8 percent interest compounded annually, at the end of five
years you will have $1,000.

Let's suppose you want to take a trip to Europe in four years and
you will need $10,000. The best interest rate you can find is 6 per-
cent. How much do you need to put in the bank today in order to be
able to take that trip? (Answer: $10,000 × 0.792 = $7,920.) We found
0.792 in the period 4 row and the 6 percent column.

Your best friend is in desperate need of some quick cash. She will
sign a promissory note for $20,000, payable in five years when the
trust fund her rich grandfather set up for her starts paying out. You

are currently earning 10 percent on your investments. How much will you loan her? (Answer: $20,000 × 0.621 = $12,420.)

Table B illustrates the present value of an annuity of $1 for different periods of time at different interest rates. We can define an annuity for these purposes as a stream of equal cash flows for a specific period of time. In other words, all of the cash flows are for the same amount. If you lease a car for $400 a month for 36 months, that is an annuity. If you mortgage a house with a fixed rate of interest for 30 years and your monthly payments are, say, $1,200, that is an annuity. If you have a variable-rate mortgage and future monthly house payments will fluctuate with changes in the interest rate, that is not an annuity. As with Table A, Table B assumes payments are made at the end of the year.

Let's see how this table works. What is the value today of receiving $1 per year for five years (a total of $5) if the appropriate interest rate is 8 percent? (Answer: $1 × 3.993 = $3.993). The annuity is $1 and the interest factor at 8 percent for five years is 3.993. The present value of an annuity is equal to the amount of each annuity payment times the interest factor for a given rate of interest and period of time. (PV Annuity = Annuity Payment × Interest Factor.)

If you put $3.993 in the bank today at 8 percent interest, compounded annually, beginning one year from now you can begin drawing out $1 per year for five years. At the end of the fifth year both your principal and earned interest will have been drawn out and your bank balance will be zero.

What is the value today of receiving $5,000 per year, beginning one year from now for 20 years if you can earn 12 percent on your investment? (Answer: $5,000 × 7.469 = $37,345.) What if you can only earn 8 percent on your investment? (Answer $5,000 × 9.818 = $49,090.)

If you examine these two tables closely you will discover that Table B (Present Value of Annuity) is merely the cumulative of Table A (Present Value of $1.00). Add the amounts in any column for any interest rate and then compare your result with the corresponding interest rate and amount of time in Table B. The numbers will be the same.

Capital Investment Decision Models

There are several different decision models we can use to evaluate proposed capital projects. We want to consider three and mention a fourth. The three that deserve most of our attention are net present value, internal rate of return and the payback period. It should be noted that these are not competing methods. Each has its individual strengths and one is not inherently better than the others. Nor is it a matter of using one versus the others. If you are going to make a capital expenditure decision involving a large amount of money, it only makes sense to look at it from different perspectives. The fourth model we will discuss is the accounting rate of return. It is not generally thought to be as good a model for decision making. We mention it only because, even with its faults, it is still fairly widely used.

Net Present Value (NPV)

To calculate a capital project's NPV, we need to first forecast the amount and timing of the cash inflows and outflows associated with the project and then, using the appropriate discount rate, determine the present value of these cash flows. As we will shortly see, using different interest rates will result in different net present values. If the present value of the expected cash inflows is greater than the present value of the expected cash outflows, the project will have a positive NPV. Everything else being equal, the firm would want to undertake a project which promised a positive NPV. Furthermore, if two mutually exclusive projects are being compared, we would want to adopt the one with the highest NPV, once again everything else being equal.

Determining the appropriate interest rate to discount future cash flows from a capital investment is beyond the scope of this book, but essentially that rate is the firm's overall cost of capital. The firm's cost of capital is the rate of return a firm must earn in order to meet its obligations and still provide the expected return to stockholders. It can be thought of as the weighted average of a firm's after-tax cost of debt and the return its stockholders are currently earning on their investment in the company. It has three components: the firm's after-tax interest rate, the firm's dividend yield and the long-term rate of stock price appreciation. Many corporate finance texts illustrate how the weighted-average cost of capital is calculated.

For many firms the cost of capital lies somewhere between 12 and 18 percent; however, this is a rather broad generalization. For our purposes we'll assume we know what the rate is. The important thing to keep in mind is that the firm's cost of capital represents a "hurdle rate." That is, if a firm invests in assets that earn less than its cost of capital, the net worth of the firm will decrease.

Internal Rate of Return (IRR)

Recall that we earlier said that using different interest rates will result in different NPVs. The higher the interest rate is, the lower the NPV of a project will be. There will be some rate of interest that results in an NPV of zero. That interest rate is the project's internal rate of return.

The present value of the cash inflows and outflows is equal when discounted at the project's IRR. Once again, everything else being equal, if the IRR of a project is greater than the firm's cost of capital, the firm would do well to undertake the project. Likewise, if we are faced with mutually exclusive projects we would select the one with the highest IRR.

Payback Period

The payback period of a capital investment is the time it takes to recoup the initial investment in terms of cash flows, that is, when the total cash inflows of an investment equal the total cash outflows. We can calculate a simple payback period where we do not discount future cash flows. We can also calculate a discounted payback period where we do.

* * * * *

Let's illustrate the estimation of cash flows and the use of these decision models with the following example.

Soonco, Inc. is considering the purchase of a machine which costs $100,000. The cost of transportation in, installation and employee

training is estimated to be an additional $20,000. Management esti-
mates the machine will provide annual before-tax cash savings of
$40,000 per year. The machine has an estimated life of five years
and a zero salvage value. Soonco will depreciate the machine over
its expected useful life using the straight-line method. Soonco, Inc.'s
cost of capital is 12 percent, and it faces a 40 percent tax rate. Is the
present value of the machine's projected cash flows greater than the
present value of its cash outflows if discounted at 12 percent? What
are the NPV, IRR and payback period of this investment? Should
the company make the investment?

The first step in answering these questions is to calculate the cash
flows associated with Soonco's proposed investment. We know the
initial cash outflow will include the purchase price and the other
costs involved in getting the machine in place and ready to operate.
These will total $120,000. The annual cash inflows are calculated as
follows:

Annual before-tax cash savings	$40,000
Less annual depreciation ($120,000 ÷ 5)	24,000
Increase in annual taxable income	16,000
Less increase in tax expense ($16,000 × 0.40)	6,400
Increase in annual income	9,600
Add back annual depreciation	24,000
Annual cash flow from investment	$33,600

Let's talk for a minute about the treatment of depreciation in these
calculations. Note that the $33,600 cash flow is simply the annual
cash savings minus taxes ($40,000 − $6,400). Why then did we first
subtract depreciation and later add it back in? Recall that depreciation is a non-cash expense that is tax deductible. We first deducted
depreciation in order to calculate the change in taxable income so
we could calculate Soonco's tax expense – a decidedly cash expense.
Since depreciation, however, is a non-cash expense, we added it back
in order to determine the project's impact on cash flow.

We have now estimated Soonco's initial cash outlay and its annual cash inflows. Because Soonco's cost of capital is 12 percent, we want to use that rate to determine the present value of these cash flows.

Looking at Figure 5.2, we see the heading "Period" and then numbers running from 0 to 5. These numbers represent the years of the expected useful life of the asset. Year 0 represents the present time. We multiply the respective cash flows by the appropriate interest factor. The appropriate interest factor for period zero (the present) is always 1.0 regardless of the interest rate at which the cash flows are discounted.

If you are comfortable with Microsoft's Excel program, use it to calculate a project's NPV. It is not as intuitive as the chart, but once you are familiar with Excel it is much easier and quicker to use. To illustrate its use in solving this problem, open the Excel program and in the function box type in =PV(12%,5,-33600). That is 12 percent discount rate, five-year life and annual cash flows of $33,600. Hit Enter and you will see $121,120. Subtract the initial cash outflow of $120,000 and the result is $1,120. This is the present value of the cash inflows. (The $8 difference is due to rounding.) Nothing could be simpler.

As our calculations indicate, Soonco's proposed project has a net present value of $1,128. Should they accept this opportunity? Well,

Net Present Value Calculation (12%)						
Period	0	1	2	3	4	5
Initial outlay	($120,000)					
Annual C/F		$33,600	$33,600	$33,600	$33,600	$33,600
Interest factor (12%)		1.0	0.893	0.797	0.712	0.636	0.567
Present value	($120,000)	$30,005	$26,779	$23,923	$21,370	$19,051
Net present value of project at 12% = $1,128						

Figure 5.2

maybe yes, but they're probably not going to be overly excited about it. Their return will exceed their cost of capital (12 percent), but not by much. Is it really enough to make the investment? How confident are they in their cost projections? What if the estimate of cash flows five years out is off by only $2,000? What is management's attitude toward risk? What about the growth of technology? Will this machine become technologically obsolete within five years? Will a better opportunity present itself in six months?

At this point in the decision-making process Soonco's management might want to look at some factors that can sometimes be hard to quantify. What impact will this decision have on their labor force, their suppliers, the environment, the quality of their product or service and so on?

What if Soonco's cost of capital was 10 percent instead of 12 percent? If we discount the project's expected cash flows using a rate of 10 percent will the project offer a greater or smaller net present value than at 12 percent? The analysis is shown in Figure 5.3.

As we saw in the first example the cash flows forecasted for this project indicate a return just slightly over 12 percent. That is why its NPV was quite low when the cash flows were discounted at 12 percent. If Soonco are currently earning an average return on their

Net Present Value Calculation (10%)						
Period	0	1	2	3	4	5
Initial outlay	($120,000)					
Annual C/F		33,600	$33,600	$33,600	$33,600	$33,600
Interest factor (10%)	1.0	0.909	0.826	0.751	0.683	0.621
Present value	($120,000)	$30,542	$27,754	$25,234	$22,949	$20,866
Net present value of project at 10% = $7,345						

Figure 5.3

assets of only 10 percent, an asset that helps them earn 12 percent will obviously increase their overall return and will subsequently increase the value of the firm. By how much will the firm's net worth be increased? Figure 5.3 indicates $7,345. You can verify this number by using Excel as we did in the first example.

A firm's cost of capital becomes the "hurdle" rate for proposed investments. Investments that make it over the hurdle are the ones we want to make, everything else being equal. When we used 12 percent as Soonco's cost of capital and discounted the cash flows at that rate, we were very ambivalent about whether or not we wanted to make the investment. When we assumed that Soonco had a cost of capital of only 10 percent, we found that the investment was a lot more attractive.

Let's go one step further with this example. What if Soonco's cost of capital was 14 percent? Our analysis is shown in Figure 5.4.

If we discount the cash flows from this project at 14 percent, it will have a negative cash flow of $4,652. If Soonco currently have a cost of capital of 14 percent, they would not want to make this investment. To do so would decrease their overall return and would reduce the value of the firm correspondingly. At 14 percent, this project does not pass muster.

* * * * *

Net Present Value Calculation (14%)						
Period/	0	1	2	3	4	5
Initial outlay	($120,000)					
Annual C/F		$33,600	$33,600	$33,600	$33,600	$33,600
Interest factor (14%)	1.0	0.877	0.770	0.675	0.592	0.519
Present value	($120,000)	$29,467	$25,872	$22,680	$19,891	$17,438
Net present value of project at 14% = ($4,652)						

Figure 5.4

We have now looked at the project using three different discount rates. The NPV of the project was positive at 10 percent, negative at 14 percent and positive, but barely so, at 12 percent. Within 1 percent, what would you estimate the internal rate of return to be? If you ballparked that number somewhere between 12 and 13 percent, you were right. Following the directions for your calculator or using Excel, calculate the IRR.

If you use Excel, type =RATE(5,-33600,120,000) in the function box. You will find the IRR to be 12.4 percent. The IRR of an investment is the actual yield (return) it provides. It is the interest rate that equates the stream of cash outflows and inflows. If the IRR of a project is greater than the firm's cost of capital, make the investment.

Answer these questions. How old is the cell phone you use – over two years old? You've probably been thinking it's time to get a new one. How old is the computer you use every day – over three years old? You've been looking to upgrade, haven't you? Your cell phone and computer haven't worn out. They probably work just as well today as when you took them out of the box. But they are on the cusp of becoming technologically obsolete. They don't have all the bells and whistles that the newer models have. Given the rate of technological growth, it is more important now than ever for organizations to consider the useful, technological lifespan of their investments.

The payback method measures the time required for a capital investment to break even in terms of cash flow. This method is often criticized for not taking the time value of money into account, although it is easy to take into account, as shown in the following paragraphs. It is also found wanting for not taking into account cash flows that occur after the payback period. The reality is, however, that it is widely used and for good reason.

How long will it take for Soonco to recoup their investment in terms of cash flow? In other words, what is the project's payback period? If we don't bother to discount the cash flows, the payback period is simply the project's initial cash flow divided by annual cash inflows ($120,000 ÷ $33,600 = 3.57 years).

If we use discounted cash flows, we can subtract them from the original investment until we hit zero. The payback period for this project if we use a 12 percent discount rate is $120,000 − $30,005 − $26,779 − $23,923 − $21,370 = $17,923 (years zero through four). The present value of year five cash flow is $19,051. So the payback period is going to be almost five years when we adjust cash flows for their present value.

What will the discounted payback period be if we use a 10 percent discount rate? 14 percent?

Accounting Rate of Return (ARR)

The ARR is often used when making capital investment decisions. However, in most cases it shouldn't be. There are two main reasons why it is a poor method to use. First, it relies on measures of income and not cash flows. We have seen that income figures often rely on estimates and arbitrary allocations. Consequently, they are subject to manipulation. On the other hand, cash flows are real. They are far more objective and are not nearly so easy to manipulate. The second reason is that ARR does not take into account the time value of money. It gives the same weight to income earned in future years as it does to current income.

The ARR of a proposed project is calculated as the average after-tax income from the investment divided by its average book value. Average book value is simply the beginning book value of the project's assets plus their ending book value divided by two. In our example for Soonco, the average after-tax income is $9,600. The average book value is ($120,000 + 0) ÷ 2 = $60,000. The ARR of this project is therefore $9,600 ÷ $60,000 = 16 percent.

Despite its potential for abuses and misuses, ARR is widely used. At this point the curious reader might ask why. The answer is, managers are often evaluated on the basis of their division's return on investment (ROI). Their promotions and year-end bonuses are often determined on their unit's ROI.

Consider this not uncommon scenario: You're a bright young manager with ambitions and hopes of earning a comfortable income and climbing the corporate ladder of success at Soonco. You've gotten off to a great start since graduating college and are considered a rising star. Your division is currently earning a return on investment of 25 percent. This is considerably higher than Soonco's overall average ARR of 16 percent. You have been presented with the following investment opportunity: required investment, $100,000; expected life of investment, five years; projected annual income, $10,000. The accounting rate of return is $10,000 ÷ [($100,000 + 0)]/2 = 20 percent.

Will you take advantage of this investment opportunity? If you do, it will lower your division's return because the return from the investment is lower than what you are currently earning (20 percent versus 25 percent). You will probably have a strong incentive to not make the investment. Should you make the investment? If you do, it will increase the corporation's overall return. Stockholders would like that. It's a bit of a conundrum, isn't it?

Summary

The essential difference between short-term and long-term decisions lies in the fact that there is a time value to money. In the short term the time value can be ignored; in the long term it cannot.

In order to evaluate long-term decisions it is first necessary to estimate the amount and timing of future cash flows. This chapter illustrates the process of estimating cash flows and two different methods (present value tables and Excel) of determining the present value of these cash flows.

Four different capital budgeting models are presented. These are net present value, internal rate of return, payback period and accounting rate of return. NPV and IRR use discounted cash flows to evaluate proposals. The payback method calculates the length of time it will take a capital investment to recover the initial and any subsequent cash outflows. ARR does not use cash flows, but relies on accounting income numbers in its calculations.

Exercises

1   Why is it important to consider the time value of money when making capital budgeting decisions?

2   How does depreciation affect cash flows?

3   What is the present value of receiving $500 per year for five years if your required rate of return is 12 percent?

4   What is the present value of receiving $500 in five years if your required rate of return is 12 percent?

5   Kathy Smith is considering the purchase of a cost-saving machine that costs $100,000. She expects to save $30,000 per year for five years. At the end of the fifth year the machine will have no salvage value and will be scrapped. What is the NPV of the machine if Kathy's cost of capital is 8 percent? (Ignore income taxes.)

6   What are the IRR and the payback period of Kathy Smith's proposed purchase?

7   What subjective factors might Kathy want to consider when making her decision?

8   Bijou, Inc. is considering the purchase of a bus to take tourists on sightseeing tours. The bus will cost $80,000. Annual cash costs of running the bus are estimated to be $30,000. Annual revenues are estimated to be $70,000. The bus has an estimated useful life of four years, after which it will have no appreciable sales value. Bijou, Inc. will depreciate the bus using the straight-line method and faces a 30 percent tax rate.

   (a) What are the annual cash flows from this investment?
   (b) What is the project's NPV if Bijou, Inc. has a 10 percent cost of capital?
   (c) What is the discounted payback period?
   (d) What is the project's ARR?
   (e) Should Bijou, Inc. undertake this investment?

DECISION MAKING II

Appendix to Chapter 5

Present Value Tables

Table A: Present Value of $1

Periods	1%	2%	3%	4%	5%	6%	7%	8%	9%
1	0.990	0.980	0.971	0.962	0.952	0.943	0.935	0.926	0.917
2	0.980	0.961	0.943	0.925	0.907	0.890	0.873	0.857	0.842
3	0.971	0.942	0.915	0.889	0.864	0.840	0.816	0.794	0.772
4	0.961	0.924	0.888	0.855	0.823	0.792	0.763	0.735	0.708
5	0.951	0.906	0.883	0.822	0.784	0.747	0.713	0.681	0.650
6	0.942	0.888	0.837	0.790	0.746	0.705	0.666	0.630	0.596
7	0.933	0.871	0.813	0.760	0.711	0.665	0.623	0.583	0.547
8	0.923	0.853	0.789	0.731	0.677	0.627	0.582	0.540	0.502
9	0.914	0.837	0.766	0.703	0.645	0.592	0.544	0.500	0.460
10	0.905	0.820	0.744	0.676	0.614	0.558	0.508	0.463	0.422
11	0.896	0.804	0.722	0.650	0.585	0.527	0.475	0.429	0.388
12	0.887	0.788	0.701	0.625	0.557	0.497	0.444	0.397	0.356
13	0.879	0.773	0.681	0.601	0.530	0.469	0.415	0.368	0.326
14	0.870	0.758	0.661	0.577	0.505	0.442	0.388	0.340	0.299
15	0.861	0.743	0.642	0.555	0.481	0.417	0.362	0.315	0.275
16	0.853	0.728	0.623	0.534	0.458	0.394	0.339	0.292	0.252
17	0.844	0.714	0.605	0.513	0.436	0.371	0.317	0.270	0.231
18	0.836	0.700	0.587	0.494	0.416	0.350	0.296	0.250	0.212
19	0.828	0.686	0.570	0.475	0.396	0.331	0.277	0.232	0.194
20	0.820	0.673	0.554	0.456	0.377	0.312	0.258	0.215	0.178
21	0.811	0.660	0.538	0.439	0.359	0.294	0.242	0.199	0.164
22	0.803	0.647	0.522	0.422	0.342	0.278	0.226	0.184	0.150
23	0.795	0.634	0.507	0.406	0.326	0.262	0.211	0.170	0.138
24	0.788	0.622	0.492	0.390	0.310	0.247	0.197	0.158	0.126
25	0.780	0.610	0.478	0.375	0.295	0.233	0.184	0.146	0.116
26	0.772	0.598	0.464	0.361	0.281	0.220	0.172	0.135	0.106
27	0.764	0.586	0.450	0.347	0.268	0.207	0.161	0.125	0.098
28	0.757	0.574	0.437	0.333	0.255	0.196	0.150	0.116	0.090
29	0.749	0.563	0.424	0.321	0.243	0.185	0.141	0.107	0.082
30	0.742	0.552	0.412	0.308	0.231	0.174	0.131	0.099	0.075
40	0.672	0.453	0.307	0.208	0.142	0.097	0.067	0.046	0.032
50	0.608	0.372	0.228	0.141	0.087	0.054	0.034	0.021	0.013

Table A (continued): Present Value of $1

Periods	10%	12%	14%	15%	16%	18%	20%	25%	30%
1	0.909	0.893	0.877	0.870	0.862	0.847	0.833	0.800	0.769
2	0.826	0.797	0.769	0.756	0.743	0.718	0.694	0.640	0.592
3	0.751	0.712	0.675	0.658	0.641	0.609	0.579	0.512	0.455
4	0.683	0.636	0.592	0.572	0.552	0.516	0.482	0.410	0.350
5	0.621	0.567	0.519	0.497	0.476	0.437	0.402	0.328	0.269
6	0.564	0.507	0.456	0.432	0.410	0.370	0.335	0.262	0.207

7	0.513	0.452	0.400	0.376	0.354	0.314	0.279	0.210	0.159
8	0.467	0.404	0.351	0.327	0.305	0.266	0.233	0.168	0.123
9	0.424	0.361	0.308	0.284	0.263	0.225	0.194	0.134	0.094
10	0.386	0.322	0.270	0.247	0.227	0.191	0.162	0.107	0.073
11	0.350	0.287	0.237	0.215	0.195	0.162	0.135	0.086	0.056
12	0.319	0.257	0.208	0.187	0.168	0.137	0.112	0.069	0.043
13	0.290	0.229	0.182	0.163	0.145	0.116	0.093	0.055	0.033
14	0.263	0.205	0.160	0.141	0.125	0.099	0.078	0.044	0.025
15	0.239	0.183	0.140	0.123	0.108	0.084	0.065	0.035	0.020
16	0.218	0.163	0.123	0.107	0.093	0.071	0.054	0.028	0.015
17	0.198	0.146	0.108	0.093	0.080	0.060	0.045	0.023	0.012
18	0.180	0.130	0.095	0.081	0.069	0.051	0.038	0.018	0.009
19	0.164	0.116	0.083	0.070	0.060	0.043	0.031	0.014	0.007
20	0.149	0.104	0.073	0.061	0.051	0.037	0.026	0.012	0.005
21	0.135	0.093	0.064	0.053	0.044	0.031	0.022	0.009	0.004
22	0.123	0.083	0.056	0.046	0.038	0.026	0.018	0.007	0.003
23	0.112	0.074	0.049	0.040	0.033	0.022	0.015	0.006	0.002
24	0.102	0.066	0.043	0.035	0.028	0.019	0.013	0.005	0.002
25	0.092	0.059	0.038	0.030	0.024	0.016	0.010	0.004	0.001
26	0.084	0.053	0.033	0.026	0.021	0.014	0.009	0.003	0.001
27	0.076	0.047	0.029	0.023	0.018	0.011	0.007	0.002	0.001
28	0.069	0.042	0.026	0.020	0.016	0.010	0.006	0.002	0.001
29	0.063	0.037	0.022	0.017	0.014	0.008	0.005	0.002	
30	0.057	0.033	0.020	0.015	0.012	0.007	0.004	0.001	
40	0.022	0.011	0.005	0.004	0.003	0.001	0.001		
50	0.009	0.003	0.001	0.001	0.001				

Table B: Present Value of Annuity of $1

Periods	1%	2%	3%	4%	5%	6%	7%	8%	9%
1	0.990	0.980	0.971	0.962	0.952	0.943	0.935	0.926	0.917
2	1.970	1.942	1.913	1.886	1.859	1.833	1.808	1.783	1.759
3	2.941	2.884	2.829	2.775	2.723	2.673	2.624	2.577	2.531
4	3.902	3.808	3.717	3.630	3.546	3.465	3.387	3.312	3.240
5	4.853	4.713	4.580	4.452	4.329	4.212	4.100	3.993	3.890
6	5.795	5.601	5.417	5.242	5.076	4.917	4.767	4.623	4.486
7	6.728	6.472	6.230	6.002	5.786	5.582	5.389	5.206	5.033
8	7.652	7.325	7.020	6.733	6.463	6.210	5.971	5.747	5.535
9	8.566	8.162	7.786	7.435	7.108	6.802	6.515	6.247	5.995
10	9.471	8.983	8.530	8.111	7.722	7.360	7.024	6.710	6.418
11	10.368	9.787	9.253	8.760	8.306	7.887	7.499	7.139	6.805
12	11.255	10.575	9.954	9.385	8.863	8.384	7.943	7.536	7.161
13	12.134	11.348	10.635	9.986	9.394	8.853	8.358	7.904	7.487
14	13.004	12.106	11.296	10.563	9.899	9.295	8.745	8.244	7.786
15	13.865	12.849	11.938	11.118	10.380	9.712	9.108	8.559	8.061
16	14.718	13.578	12.561	11.652	10.838	10.106	9.447	8.851	8.313
17	15.562	14.292	13.166	12.166	11.274	10.477	9.763	9.122	8.544
18	16.398	14.992	13.754	12.659	11.690	10.828	10.059	9.372	8.756
19	17.226	15.678	14.324	13.134	12.085	11.158	10.336	9.604	8.950

20	18.046	16.351	14.878	13.590	12.462	11.470	10.594	9.818	9.129
21	18.857	17.011	15.415	14.029	12.821	11.764	10.836	10.017	9.292
22	19.660	17.658	15.937	14.451	13.163	12.042	11.061	10.201	9.442
23	20.456	18.292	16.444	14.857	13.489	12.303	11.272	10.371	9.580
24	21.243	18.914	16.936	15.247	13.799	12.550	11.469	10.529	9.707
25	22.023	19.523	17.413	15.622	14.094	12.783	11.654	10.675	9.823
26	22.795	20.121	17.877	15.983	14.375	13.003	11.826	10.810	9.929
27	23.560	20.707	18.327	16.330	14.643	13.211	11.987	10.935	10.027
28	24.316	21.281	18.764	16.663	14.898	13.406	12.137	11.051	10.116
29	25.066	21.844	19.189	16.984	15.141	13.591	12.278	11.158	10.198
30	25.808	22.396	19.600	17.292	15.373	13.765	12.409	11.258	10.274
40	32.835	27.355	23.115	19.793	17.159	15.046	13.332	11.925	10.757
50	39.196	31.424	25.730	21.482	18.256	15.762	13.801	12.234	10.962

Table B (continued): Present Value of Annuity of $1

Periods	10%	12%	14%	15%	16%	18%	20%	25%	30%
1	0.909	0.893	0.877	0.870	0.862	0.847	0.833	0.800	0.769
2	1.736	1.690	1.647	1.626	1.605	1.566	1.528	1.440	1.361
3	2.487	2.402	2.322	2.283	2.246	2.174	2.106	1.952	1.816
4	3.170	3.037	2.914	2.855	2.798	2.690	2.589	2.362	2.166
5	3.791	3.605	3.433	3.352	3.274	3.127	2.991	2.689	2.436
6	4.355	4.111	3.889	3.784	3.685	3.498	3.326	2.951	2.643
7	4.868	4.564	4.288	4.160	4.039	3.812	3.605	3.161	2.802
8	5.335	4.968	4.639	4.487	4.344	4.078	3.837	3.329	2.925
9	5.759	5.328	4.946	4.772	4.607	4.303	4.031	3.463	3.019
10	6.145	5.650	5.216	5.019	4.833	4.494	4.192	3.571	3.092
11	6.495	5.938	5.553	5.234	5.029	4.656	4.327	3.656	3.147
12	6.814	6.194	5.660	5.421	5.197	4.793	4.439	3.725	3.190
13	7.103	6.424	5.842	5.583	5.342	4.910	4.533	3.780	3.223
14	7.367	6.628	6.002	5.724	5.468	5.008	4.611	3.824	3.249
15	7.606	6.811	6.142	5.847	5.575	5.092	4.675	3.859	3.268
16	7.824	6.974	6.265	5.954	5.669	5.162	4.730	3.887	3.283
17	8.022	7.120	6.373	6.047	5.749	5.222	4.775	3.910	3.295
18	8.201	7.250	6.467	6.128	5.818	5.273	4.812	3.928	3.304
19	8.365	7.366	6.550	6.198	5.877	5.316	4.844	3.942	3.311
20	8.514	7.469	6.623	6.259	5.929	5.353	4.870	3.954	3.316
21	8.649	7.562	6.687	6.312	5.973	5.384	4.891	3.963	3.320
22	8.772	7.645	6.743	6.359	6.011	5.410	4.909	3.970	3.323
23	8.883	7.718	6.792	6.399	6.044	5.432	4.925	3.976	3.325
24	8.985	7.784	6.835	6.434	6.073	5.451	4.937	3.981	3.327
25	9.077	7.843	6.873	6.464	6.097	5.467	4.948	3.985	3.329
26	9.161	7.896	6.906	6.491	6.118	5.480	4.956	3.988	3.330
27	9.237	7.943	6.935	6.514	6.136	5.492	4.964	3.990	3.331
28	9.307	7.984	6.961	6.534	6.152	5.502	4.970	3.992	3.331
29	9.370	8.022	6.983	6.551	6.166	5.510	4.975	3.994	3.332
30	9.427	8.055	7.003	6.566	6.177	5.517	4.979	3.995	3.332
40	9.779	8.244	7.105	6.642	6.234	5.548	4.997	3.999	3.333
50	9.915	8.305	7.133	6.661	6.246	5.554	4.999	4.000	3.333

6

PLANNING AND BUDGETING

Zeus does not bring all men's plans to fulfillment.

(Homer, *Iliad*, XVII)

It's a bad plan that admits of no modification.

(Publilius Syrus, Maxim 469)

Chapter Overview

This chapter discusses the importance of organizations' operating budgets and illustrates how they are created. After studying the chapter you should:

- Understand the importance of budgeting;
- Understand the mechanics of putting together an organization's master operating budget;
- Understand how the various elements of an organization's income statement affect its balance sheet and its needs for financing.

* * * * *

As a manager, a lot of your time probably involves four major activities: planning, organizing, controlling and directing. Accounting plays a central role in each of these activities. It does so largely through the budgeting process. An organization's operating budget is a plan of action or, more precisely, a quantified plan of action. It communicates the firm's goals and sets forth expectations in financial terms. It helps answer such questions as: What level of sales will we need this year to achieve our desired rate of return? What are our budgeted costs? Which costs are fixed and which are variable? The budget can also provide an estimate of the resources and funding a firm will need to achieve its operating goals.

Not only is the budget a valuable planning tool, it also serves as a control device by setting limits and expectations for managers and employees. A properly prepared budget provides an organization with an effective tool to monitor and control operations and spending. For example, an operating budget will show how the amount and timing of an organization's sales affect its production schedule, its schedule for purchasing raw materials and its human resource needs.

You cannot effectively organize resources and activities without this type of planning. Managing without an operating budget is a bit like driving around without a map and unsure of your destination but hoping you get there on time without running out of gas. Budgeting acts as a compass. It provides direction, focus and a means of control. Just the act of going through the budgeting process forces you to identify and analyze the relationships between the various elements of your organization.

Before we go further, let's make clear that accountants do not "own" the budget or the budgeting process. No one individual or office does. Budgeting is by necessity an interdisciplinary group process. The proper role of accounting is to organize and coordinate the process and to crunch the numbers. Most of the relevant input should come from marketing, engineering, production and anyone else who has knowledge of, and insight into, the firm's goals and how the firm operates.

Budgets provide a guide for expected performance and, if prepared and used properly, can serve as a powerful means of communication and motivation. Together with financial statements, budgets can influence the behavior and daily lives of people in all sorts of organizations. The daily activities of managers and other employees are often directed toward meeting sales and production quotas and controlling costs in order to meet budgeted results. Promotions, bonuses and job security are often based on achieving budgeted accounting numbers.

If this behavioral aspect goes unrecognized, budgets can also serve to un-motivate personnel and lead to dysfunctional behavior. If budget standards are set too high, the typical argument is that employees become frustrated and do not attempt to achieve them. "If we're going to have an unfavorable variance no matter what we do, why should we even try?" There are empirical studies to back this assertion, and it also seems intuitive.[1]

On the other hand, if standards are set too low, employees will merely work to the level of expectations. "There's no need to work harder than the boss expects us to." Once again, the argument has a certain intuitive appeal. Clearly, setting the budget at appropriate levels and with buy-in from all constituents is key to effective operations.

Ideally the budget will provide for goal congruence. The notion of goal congruence is often misunderstood. It does *not* mean that employees subordinate their personal goals to those of the organization. That is an unrealistic notion. No rational person is going to go to work on a daily basis putting the well-being of faceless stockholders ahead of the well-being of his or her family or self. Goal congruence means that people working in their own enlightened self-interest do so in such a manner that their goals are coincident with those of the organization. By achieving their personal goals they will also further those of the organization. This, for example, is why commissions based on profit margins often make up a significant part of salespersons' income and why production personnel are rewarded for achieving production and efficiency goals.

Budgets also provide information necessary for control. In order to control anything, whether it is a firm's operations, an airplane or the temperature in the room, a control system needs two pieces of information: where we are and where we should be. The firm's financial statements tell managers where the firm is, that is, what the sales, expenses, assets, liabilities and owners' equity are. The budget tells managers what these should be if they are to be in line with the firm's goals.

Putting a budget together involves more than having some vague notion of where we want to go. It requires that we have specific goals, plans and times regarding how and when to achieve those goals. To be effective, it also requires some flexibility.

Developing the Operating Budget

The mechanics of developing a master operating budget involve putting together a set of pro forma, or projected, financial statements and supporting schedules. Budgeting is a bit like working a jigsaw puzzle. It involves putting a lot of pieces of the budgeting puzzle together and seeing if they fit and if they will work satisfactorily. If they don't we'll have to go back and move the pieces around and substitute new pieces in place of the old.

An organization's marketing department is absolutely central to the budgeting process. Budgeting begins with a market forecast. We need to know what products or services we are going to sell, how much of each we will sell, at what price we expect to sell them, and when we will sell them. (It's important to know if we are going to sell those widgets in February or in September.) The level and timing of expected future sales are usually the most important factors that drive an organization's activities and determine the amount and timing of the resources it will need.

There is a hierarchy involved in putting together the operating budget. Once the market forecast has been delivered and agreed upon, the engineering, production and service departments can determine which activities must take place and what resources the firm will need, and when they will be needed, in order to fulfill the sales forecast. Once the required needs and timing have been determined the purchasing department can lay plans to have the right amount of the right materials on hand at the right time in order to satisfy production needs. Likewise, the human resource department will be in a position to establish human resource needs, noting when vacations can be taken, when and if lay-offs may be necessary, and when and if temporary workers might need to be hired or overtime scheduled.

Putting a budget together requires that participants understand the firm's production, marketing and distribution processes, how they interact and relate to one another and how the interaction of these processes determines the success of the firm. Admittedly, the more people involved in the budgeting process, the more cumbersome it becomes, but involving more people leads to wider understanding. If you're in charge of putting next year's operating budget together, you'll be well advised to get input from as many people as you can, including the worker on the factory floor, the clerk in the warehouse, the administrative assistant or the law clerk. They know things you don't. Furthermore, when people are involved in a truly meaningful way, they are more inclined to take ownership in the budget and have greater motivation in achieving budgeted results.

One caveat should be offered. When putting together a budget there is a natural tendency for people to build slack into the budget. This often takes the form of underestimating future revenues, overstating budgeted costs or overstating resource needs. One way to guard against this is to benchmark a firm's budgeted results against the industry's best-practices data.

Pro Forma Income Statement

Once the marketing department has created a marketing forecast and sales revenue has been projected for the coming year, we can begin putting together the rest of the pro forma financial statements. We are, in essence, putting together a financial blueprint. We want to determine what our revenue, costs, income, resources and financing needs are going to be if we produce and sell what our marketing department tell us they think we will sell during the coming year. We will also be establishing a benchmark against which we will be able to evaluate future performance.

Consider the cost of goods sold section of the income statement. These costs consist of materials that go directly into the product or service, labor that is applied directly to the product or service (think of the guy on the assembly line, the accountant bent over your tax return or the nurse drawing blood from your arm), and overhead (taxes, rent, insurance, depreciation, utilities, etc.).

Based on the forecast of how many units of the various products we are going to sell, we can estimate how much direct material and direct labor we're going to need, when we will need them, and how much they will cost. Direct material and direct labor are examples of engineered costs. That is, they are engineered or designed into the product.

Forecasting problems often arise when direct materials involve a commodity like oil where prices can fluctuate greatly over the course of a year. In situations such as this, budgets will need to be periodically adjusted to reflect current economic conditions.

Budgeting for overhead costs is a bit more involved because these costs are not engineered into the product. Overhead generally relates to a firm's capacity. A firm with a large capacity will generally have higher overhead costs than one with smaller capacity. That is, a larger firm will likely have greater rent expense, depreciation, taxes, insurance and so on.

Here's one way to estimate overhead for the coming year. Analyze the individual accounts that make up overhead. Determine which accounts contain costs that remain fixed regardless of the level of output. Unless the cost of something like rent, property tax or insurance has changed, the cost next year will be pretty much the same as last. If one of these fixed costs is to increase, your landlord or agent is going to let you know. If that is the case, use the new data.

Variable overhead costs, as their name implies, vary with output. Estimating what these might be is not so straightforward. Our job here is to find out the rate at which these costs vary with output. Some will vary proportionately, some more, some less. To determine the rate at which these costs vary, segregate the variable costs from the fixed and then collect production data for the past several years. Once you've done this you can then apply regression analysis to determine how the variable costs change in relation to changes in output. Regression analysis is beyond the scope of this book, but basic statistics books can lead you through the process step by step, and the Microsoft Excel program makes it rather painless.

Once we have estimated the future cost of goods sold we are in a position to estimate gross profit and move on to selling, general and administrative expenses. Estimating these is much the same as estimating future costs of goods sold. These expenses tend to fall into one of three categories: variable, fixed or discretionary. To forecast variable and fixed expenses, we will need to analyze their behavior over a period of several years and apply the same methods we used in forecasting overhead costs.

Discretionary costs fall into a different category. Discretionary costs amount to what they do solely because management decided, at its discretion, to allot that much. Examples of discretionary expenses include such things as advertising, maintenance and management training. In any given year, management can increase or decrease the amount they spend for these purposes.

Other items such as future interest expense and taxes should be fairly easy to calculate. Interest expense will simply depend on the firm's current debt and the interest rate on that debt plus amounts expected to be borrowed at the going interest rate. Once we forecast income for the coming period we can apply the appropriate tax rates to calculate taxes. Extraordinary items are, of course, a wild card. Who can predict a flood or earthquake?

Pro Forma Balance Sheet

The pro forma income statement is a statement of the firm's expected activities. The pro forma balance sheet is a statement which lists the resources (assets) the firm needs to carry out those activities plus the financing (liabilities and owners' equity) of those resources. Let's take a look at the balance sheet and see how the firm's resources affect or are affected by its earnings activities.

Approximately 85 percent of American business is done on credit. An organization's normal daily operations, that is, the buying and selling of inventory and the payment of wages, rent, utilities and other expenses and liabilities, will both require and generate cash, accounts receivable and accounts payable.

To forecast the amount of cash we will have on hand or will need to borrow at a certain point in the future we need to know what our current cash balance is, our forecasted sales and the pattern of cash

receipts vis-à-vis sales, along with our payment policies with respect
to accounts payable and wages. Here's an example:

Assume we have a cash balance of $10,000 on January 1. All of
our sales are on credit and our actual sales for the prior November and December, respectively, were $30,000 and $50,000. Our
sales forecast calls for sales in January of $60,000, February $50,000
and March $70,000. In the past we have collected 60 percent of a
month's sales in the month of sale, 25 percent in the second month
and 13 percent in the third month. (The observant reader will see
that 2 percent of our sales go uncollected.) Cost of goods sold averages 50 percent of sales, and adequate merchandise inventory is purchased the month prior to sales. Wanting a good credit rating, we
are fastidious in paying for our purchases in full the month following
their purchase. Wages of $18,000 per month are paid at the end of
each month. Utilities and other expenses average $7,000 per month.
Given the above data, how much cash should we have on hand at
March 31? Our solution is below (see Table 6.1).

The important thing to note here is that an organization's daily
activities will both generate and require a certain amount of cash.

Table 6.1

Cash Collections	January	February	March	Total
From Nov. Sales	$3,900			$3,900
Dec. Sales	12,500	$6,500		19,000
Jan. Sales	36,000	15,000	$7,800	58,800
Feb. Sales		30,000	12,500	42,500
Mar. Sales			42,000	42,000
Total	$52,400	$51,500	62,300	166,200
Cash Payments				
Cost of Goods Sold	$30,000	$25,000	$35,000	$90,000
Wages	18,000	18,000	18,000	54,000
Utilities, etc.	7,000	7,000	7,000	21,000
Total	$55,000	$50,000	$51,500	$165,000
Beginning Balance	$10,000	$7,400	$8,900	$10,000
Ending Balance	$7,400	$8,900	$11,200	$11,200

In the above example our firm did not run out of cash. However, if it had been in danger of doing so, our budget forecast would have warned us of that possibility in time to get the necessary funds. Using a forecast such as this enables us to plan for those times when we will need to borrow and for those times when we can put excess cash to good use by making short-term liquid investments. Running out of cash does not do good things for a firm's credit rating, and not being able to meet payroll tends to upset employees.

The timing and amount of a firm's sales, its credit policies and the effectiveness of its credit department affect its accounts receivable balance as well as its cash. Armed with knowledge of these patterns we can estimate the balance of accounts receivable at any given time in a manner similar to that which we illustrated for estimating cash. Using the same facts as in our previous example we can forecast an accounts receivable balance at the end of the three succeeding months as follows. The January 1 balance in accounts receivable of $8,000 is assumed for illustrative purposes.

Unlike cash and accounts receivable, the amount of inventory a firm will have on hand is not automatically generated by its sales. Rather, the firm's projected sales will determine how much inventory it needs to buy or manufacture and have on hand. Also, shelf

Table 6.2

	Nov.	*Dec.*	*Jan.*	*Feb.*	*Mar.*
Sales	$30,000	$50,000	$60,000	$50,000	$70,000
Collect in month of sale (60%)			$36,000	$30,000	$42,000
Collect from one month prior (25%)			12,500	15,000	12,500
Collect from two months prior (13%)			3,900	6,500	7,800
Increase (decrease) in accounts receivable			7,600	(1,500)	7,700
Beginning balance of accounts receivable			8,000	15,600	14,100
Ending balance of accounts receivable			$15,600	14,100	$21,800

life of the inventory, lead times from suppliers, reliability of suppliers and desired safety stock, as well as the firm's philosophy regarding a just-in-time inventory policy, play a role in determining its desired level of inventory.

Moving down the pro forma balance sheet, we come to property, plant and equipment (PP&E). Unless the firm is expecting to have a major expansion, replace a large amount of aging equipment or downsize, PP&E for the coming year will probably not be significantly different next year from what the current balance sheet shows. If, however, any of these developments are in the works, then adjustments to PP&E on the pro forma statements will need to be made.

We have now made an estimate of the resources our firm's activities will either require or generate for the coming budget period. The next step in the budgeting process is to determine how we are going to finance these resources.

Once we have forecast the amount and timing of sales and created a schedule of purchases we will be in a position to forecast current liabilities. As with current assets, the firm's day-to-day operations influence the amount of these liabilities. The amount and timing of our inventory purchases, and the credit terms our suppliers offer, as well as our own payment policies, determine how much our accounts payable are at any given time. Likewise, the size of our workforce, wage rates and the length and timing of pay periods will determine the level of the wages we owe at any given time.

Short-term notes payable represent money borrowed for a relatively short period of time. Unlike accounts and wages payable, they are not the direct result of operations, but arise indirectly from past and expected future operations. Maintaining good relations and a line of credit with our bank is critical for our credit rating and our ability to borrow during those times when cash is short.

As Figure 1.4 reveals, for many firms there is often a period of time between cash outflow for inventory purchases and operating expenses and cash inflow from sales and the collection of accounts receivable. In some cases this cycle can take months. In the meantime, salaries and a myriad of other expenses need to be paid. Large inventories are usually associated with longer periods of time between cash outflows from operations and cash inflows. A just-in-time inventory policy can shorten the cycle dramatically. Operations need to be financed during the operating cycle. This financing is often done with the use of short-term notes. Forecasting short-term notes payable is often the last step in developing a pro forma balance sheet. We'll come back to them after we discuss the other items on the balance sheet.

One of the basic principles of corporate finance is that a debt's maturity should closely match the life of the asset giving rise to that debt. In other words, current debt should be incurred to finance current operations, and long-term debt should be incurred to finance long-term assets such as PP&E. When done properly, the cash flow arising from the asset can be used to liquidate the loan. This is referred to as self-liquidating financing.

If management contemplates significant increases in the firm's long-term assets, this needs to be reflected on the pro forma balance sheet along with the expected funding for these assets. Looking at Acme's balance sheet (Figure 1.3) we see that the company made relatively small increases in PP&E and long-term investments. Funds generated through current earnings were sufficient to finance the increase in these long-term assets. Consequently, Acme did not need to borrow in order to finance them. Acme was also able to generate sufficient funds through operations to pay down a portion of its long-term debt.

Forecasting stockholders' equity is relatively straightforward. Unless the firm is expecting to sell additional shares of either preferred or common stock, the amounts reported for these, along with the amount of paid-in capital in excess of par, will not change from what is shown on the previous year's balance sheet. What will change is the balance of retained earnings. Retained earnings on the pro forma balance sheet will simply be the firm's current retained earnings plus net income from the pro forma income statement minus any dividends the firm expects to pay during the coming year.

We said earlier that we would come back to short-term notes payable. Now is the time to do that. We also said that putting together the coming year's operating budget was a bit like working a jigsaw puzzle. The principle behind the balance sheet is that assets equal debt plus owners' equity. They must do so on the pro forma balance sheet as well. If the resources (assets) we will need to carry on our expected activities are greater than currently available financing, we will have to either somehow raise the difference or scale back our planned operations.

Herein lies a primary reason for putting together a budget. If we're going to have to borrow money, it's best to know that well ahead of time. Otherwise, we would have to rush to the bank at the last minute and be forced to accept unfavorable loan conditions or, worse yet, be unable to secure a loan.

Let's play out a scenario that occurs altogether too often. Let's suppose we're owners of a small, fast-growing firm and have put together a pro forma income statement, balance sheet and source and use of funds statement. We forecast strong growth and a healthy profit margin for the coming year. The pro forma balance sheet indicates we will need to borrow, say, $300,000 to carry out our planned growth. We take our last couple of years' audited financial statements to the bank along with our carefully wrought budget and make our request.

The nice loan officer says she will take our request to the bank's loan committee and will have a decision for us in two days.

We return two days later. She smiles at us and says, "I'm sorry, but the committee said 'no.'"

"Why?" we ask.

She consults her notes. "They just don't feel your firm is financially strong enough to warrant a loan of this size."

Turned down for the loan, we're disappointed. What to do? We thank her, regain our equanimity and walk out of the bank. We decide to shop for a loan at other banks. We go to two more banks and get similar responses. Why? Because most banks use similar models for making loan decisions. Of course, we're disappointed, but it is far better to be disappointed at this stage of the game than to have gone forward by buying more inventory, extending more credit and hiring more employees and then running into a cash and credit crunch. We now have the time to back up, rethink our operations and strategy and do something about it.

As we have seen, pro forma financial statements are supported by a series of secondary or sub-budgets. For example, in preparing the pro forma balance sheet we developed a cash budget. We will also have to develop a series of budgets relating to production. This is where a great deal of planning and insight into the firm's operations take place. Putting together the cash budget requires the person preparing the budget to understand how cash flows in and out of the firm. Likewise, preparing the production budget requires that one understand how labor, raw materials and overhead come together in producing the firm's product or service.

The idea behind these budgets is to ensure that we have the right amount of resources at the right time. We don't want too much cash lying around not earning a return. Then again, we don't want to be short of cash come payday. We don't want excess inventory gathering dust on the shelves and becoming obsolete or expensive equipment rusting away over in the corner. At the same time, we want adequate inventory and the capacity to manufacture that inventory or we will lose sales, contribution margins and possibly goodwill.

Illustration of Budgeting Process

Let's illustrate the budgeting process with the exercise in Figure 6.1.

What we have just done is complete the Riley Company's projected income statement for the coming year and the various schedules which support it. Along the way we made some assumptions about the expected level of sales and costs. Hopefully, we made these assumptions on the basis of sound forecasting techniques.

The Riley Company manufactures and sells one size of garden gnomes. The materials and labor to manufacture a garden gnome are:

Direct Materials:
    Resin   1 pound
    Cement   3 pounds
    (Riley considers water as part of overhead.)

Labor: 2 hours ($15/hour)

Ms. Riley expects to sell 2,000 gnomes during 2012 at a price of $100 per gnome. She anticipates the following inventory levels:

	Beginning Inventory	Ending Inventory
Finished Gnomes	200 @ $53.10	200
Resin	500 pounds ($3.00/lb)	500 pounds
Cement	1,200 pounds ($1.20/lb)	1,200 pounds

Fixed manufacturing overhead costs for the coming year are estimated to be $15,000. Variable manufacturing overhead is projected to be 30 percent of direct labor. Fixed marketing and administrative costs are estimated to be $50,000. Variable marketing and administrative costs are estimated to be 10 percent of sales. The average price of both resin and cement is expected to remain constant during the coming year. There was no work in process at either the beginning or end of 2011, and Riley expects to maintain constant inventory levels of raw materials and finished product.

Required: Prepare the following budgets for 2012: the revenue budget, production budget, direct material purchases budget, and direct labor budget. What is the total manufacturing cost of a gnome in 2012? What is the Riley Company's anticipated profit or loss for 2012?

Solution:

Revenue Budget:

Sales (2,000 gnomes × $100)	$200,000

Production Budget:

Desired ending inventory of gnomes	200
Expected sales	2,000
Total gnomes needed	2,200
Less beginning inventory of gnomes	200
Gnomes to be produced	2,000

Direct Materials Purchases Budget:

Resin:	Desired ending inventory (pounds)	500
	Needed for production (2,000 × 1)	2,000
	Total resin needed (pounds)	2,500
	Less beginning inventory of resin	500
	Pounds of resin to purchase	2,000 @ $3.00/lb = $6,000

Cement: Desired ending inventory (pounds)   1,200
         Needed for production (2,000 × 3)   6,000
         Total cement needed (pounds)   7,200
         Less beginning inventory of cement   1,200
         Pounds of cement to purchase   6,000 @ $1.20/lb = $7,200

Direct Labor Budget:

2,000 gnomes @ 2 hr/gnome × $15/hr = $60,000

Overhead Budget

Variable Overhead $0.30 per direct labor dollar 0.30 × $60,000 = $18,000
Fixed Manufacturing Overhead $15,000

Manufacturing Cost per Gnome:

Material:
    Resin   1 lb @ $3.00 $3.00
    Cement   3 lb @ $1.20   3.60
Labor   2 hr @ $15.00   30.00
Variable Overhead   0.30 × $30.00   9.00
Total Variable Manufacturing Cost per Gnome   45.60

Fixed Overhead $15,000 ÷ 2,000   7.50
    Total Manufacturing Cost per Gnome $53.10

The Riley Company
Projected Income – 2012

Sales (2,000 gnomes) $200,000
Less Cost of Goods Sold:
Beginning Finished Goods Inventory (200 @ $53.10) $10,620
Beginning Raw Materials Inventories
    Resin (500 lb @ $3.00) $1,500
    Cement (1,200 lb @ $1.20)   1,440
                                         2,940
Purchases: Resin   6,000
           Cement   7,200
Total Raw Material Available   16,140

Less Ending Raw Material Inventory		
Resin (500 lb @ $3.00)	1,500	
Cement (1,200 lb @ $1.20)	1,440	
Raw Materials Used	13,200	
Direct Labor (2 hr @ $15/hr × 2,000)	60,000	
Mfg. Overhead:		
Variable (0.30 × $60,000)	18,000	
Fixed	15,000	
Cost of Goods Manufactured		106,200
Cost of Goods Available for Sale		116,820
Less Ending Finished Goods Inventory (200 @ $53.10)		10,620
Cost of Goods Sold		106,200
Gross Profit		93,800
Less Marketing and Administrative Expenses		
Variable (0.10 × $200,000)	20,000	
Fixed	50,000	70,000
Operating Income		$23,800

Figure 6.1

A projected income statement is a statement of projected activities. We think we will have a certain level of sales, that we will use a certain amount of materials and labor, and so on. These various activities require resources, and resources need to be financed. The next step in our budgeting/planning process is to determine what those financing needs might be. We do this by projecting what our balance sheet will look like at the end of the coming year. Once again we will (or should) make these projections on the basis of sound forecasting techniques. Let's assume that we have done just that and plan for the following balances on December 31, 2012: cash $10,000; accounts receivable $8,000; property, plant and equipment (net) $110,000; accounts payable $18,000; and notes payable $12,000. Also assume that the balance in the Riley capital account was $90,000 on

January 1, 2012 and that Ms. Riley withdrew $12,000 from the company for personal use during the year. (Note: If this had been a corporation, these drawings would have been in the form of dividends to the stockholders.) To complete the planning process we need to prepare a pro forma balance sheet for December 31, 2012. It will look like this:

It doesn't take a particularly keen eye to see that the Riley Company's balance sheet doesn't balance. It is off by $9,760.00. Assets exceed liabilities and owner's equity. Have we made a mistake? The answer is no, we're just not finished quite yet. Liabilities and owner's equity represent the financing of assets. As things stand right now, the Riley Company does not have enough financing to provide the level of resources it needs to sustain the level of activities required by its income statement. To maintain the level of operations the company has budgeted for it needs to find additional financing. That is, it needs to borrow more money or Ms. Riley needs to increase her capital account by either investing more of her own funds in the company or withdrawing less for her personal use.

The Riley Company
Pro Forma Balance Sheet

Assets		Liabilities and Owner's Equity		
Cash	$ 10,000	Accounts Payable		$ 18,000
Accts Receivable	8,000	Notes Payable		12,000
Inventories*	13,560	Riley Capital		
Property (net)	110,000	Beginning balance	$ 90,000	
		Income	23,800	
		Less withdrawals	(12,000)	101,800
Totals	$ 141,560			$ 131,800

* This amount represents the total of raw materials and finished goods inventories as presented on the income statement.

Figure 6.2

Herein lies one of the main advantages of budgeting. It is far better for Ms. Riley to know well in advance that she will need to raise additional capital than to wait until she is face to face with a cash shortage. She is now in a position to go to her source of capital and negotiate more favorable loan provisions than if she had waited until a cash crunch was upon her. Her other options include cutting back on her proposed level of operations and reducing her inventory levels, thereby reducing her need for additional funds.

Summary

The goal of budgeting should be to provide the information necessary to ensure that an organization has the right amount of the right resources at the right time in order to fulfill its mission. This chapter explains the mechanics of putting together a master budget and its subsidiary budgets. It shows how the activities described in the firm's income statement affect its balance sheet and drive the need for resources and their financing.

This chapter also discusses the role budgeting plays in managerial control and stresses the need for budgets to be set at high, but attainable, standards. It is important to realize that accountants do not "own" the budgeting process. The budgeting process begins with a marketing forecast. If the forecast is not reasonably accurate, neither will be the resulting budget. Accountants may coordinate the process and crunch the numbers, but a properly prepared budget will have input from many different persons from all levels of the organization.

Exercises

1   How do budgets aid the planning process?

2   What is the main purpose of a cash budget?

3   Determine the order in which the following budgets are prepared:

(a) Budgeted balance sheet
(b) Budgeted income statement
(c) Capital expenditures budget
(d) Cash budget
(e) Operating budget
(f) Purchases and cost of goods sold budget
(g) Sales budget

4   House of the Sun Foods estimates production for the next five
    quarters as:

First quarter	20X1	50,000 meals
Second quarter	20X1	45,000 meals
Third quarter	20X1	55,000 meals
Fourth quarter	20X1	44,000 meals
First quarter	20X2	54,000 meals

Each meal requires a half-pound of beans and one pound of rice.
Beans cost $2 a pound and rice costs $3 a pound. There are
12,500 pounds of beans and 25,000 pounds of rice on hand at the
end of the fourth quarter 20X0. House of the Sun Foods wishes
to have 50 percent of next quarter's ingredients on hand at the
end of each quarter.
  Required: Prepare quarterly direct materials purchases
budgets for House of the Sun Foods for 20X1.

5   The Gisele and Edwards manufacturing company seeks to have
    a minimum $15,000 cash balance at the end of each month.
    The following amounts are given from its recent cash budget (in
    thousands). Fill in the missing amounts. (Note that the beginning
    cash balance in the total column will be the cash balance as of
    January 1.)

Table 6.3

	January	February	March	Total
Beginning cash balance	$20	?	?	$20
Collections	?	?	?	?
Total cash available	70	?	85	?
Less disbursements:				
Purchases	30	35	50	?
Operating expenses	20	?	30	?
Total disbursements	?	55	?	?
Cash balance	?	25	?	?
Balance vs. minimum ($ 15)	?	?	?	?
Borrowed				
Repaid				
Ending cash balance	$20	?	?	$15

Note

1 Jerold Zimmerman, *Accounting for Decision Making and Control*, 5th ed., New York, McGraw-Hill Irwin, 2006: 277.

7

CONTROL

Chapter Overview

This chapter discusses the difference between budgets used for planning purposes and budgets used for control purposes. It also illustrates the use of flexible budgets and variance analysis to control an organization's operations. After reading this chapter you will:

- Understand the difference between a static budget and a flexible budget;
- Understand the basic elements of a control system;
- Know how to develop a flexible budget;
- Understand the difference between volume, price and efficiency variances;
- Be able to calculate and interpret price and efficiency variances;
- Be able to calculate and interpret variable overhead variances;
- Understand how to use variance analysis for control purposes.

* * * * *

"The best laid plans of mice and men go oft astray" (Robert Burns, 1785) – especially if your control system is not up to the task. All the planning and budgeting we talked about in the previous chapter will be of little value if an organization cannot control its operations and costs.

Whether you want to control product costs, production quality, the temperature in your office, the direction and speed of your car or your temper, you need a control system. Control systems have three components:

1   A feedback device that provides information about your current situation, that is, where you are, how fast you're going, what your blood pressure is and so on.
2   Information about what your current situation should be, for example standard costs, budgeted revenues, normal blood pressure and so on.
3   A means of getting from where you are to where you should be.

Think of the thermostat on the wall in your living room. Its thermometer tells you what the current temperature is. If you don't like the current temperature you can adjust the thermostat's dial to one that is more comfortable. If the room temperature reads below the desired level you have selected, an electrical connection is made and the furnace kicks in. When the desired temperature is reached, the electrical connection is broken and the furnace shuts off. It is a very simple, very clever, very effective control device.

For the purposes of controlling your organization's operations and costs, financial statements tell you where you are and the budget tells you where you want to be. Remember, however, that when we earlier talked about budgets we did so in the context of planning. We created static, before-the-fact planning devices. We were budgeting for a specific level of sales. Chances are our actual level of sales and other results will be somewhat different than what we had originally budgeted.

Static budgets are great for planning purposes, but not necessarily so for control. If we do not achieve our exact projected level of sales, a static budget will not provide the information we need to compare what we did with what we should have done. Therefore it will not provide the information we need to control operations and costs. For control purposes, we need to modify our budget into a more flexible form.

Flexible Budgets

This chapter introduces the concept of flexible budgets. A flexible budget differs from a static budget in several ways. A static budget is based on standard revenues and costs per unit of our product or service and the **planned** level of output. A flexible budget, on the other hand, is based on standard revenues and costs per unit and the **actual** level of output. Preparing a flexible budget begins with determining which costs and revenues are fixed and which are variable. Consider the following example, which uses data from the Riley Company. Recall from Chapter 6 that its budgeted income statement for the coming year was as shown in Figure 7.1.

The Riley Company didn't quite make its budgeted profit. Its actual income statement for the year is presented in Figure 7.2.

The Riley Company's actual sales were 4 percent higher than budget, yet its operating income was off by 21 percent. What went wrong? Let's take a look.

Different Layers of Analysis

Comparing actual to budget data for control purposes is a bit like peeling an onion. We can do it in layers. Merely comparing budgeted and actual income is not going to give us any real insight into our firm's operations. It doesn't tell us how well we did with respect to generating revenues or controlling costs. A deeper level of analysis can be gained by comparing the two income statements line by line.

This level of analysis (shown in Figure 7.3) provides considerably more information than merely comparing actual profits to budgeted profits. In this case we see that actual revenues exceeded planned by $8,000. In addition to a few smaller variances, the Riley Company used $1,080 more raw materials than planned, paid $6,375 more in wages and wound up with $2,655 less in ending finished goods inventory than the static budget called for.

We are still, however, left with some major questions. What led to the sales variance of $8,000? Was it because they sold more units or because they sold their product at a higher price than the original budget called for? Or was it some combination of the two? Likewise,

The Riley Company
Projected Income – 2012

Sales (2,000 gnomes @ $100)		$200,000
Less Cost of Goods Sold:		
Beginning Finished Goods Inventory (200 @ $53.10)		$10,620
Beginning Raw Materials Inventories		
Resin (500 lb @ $3.00)	$1,500	
Cement (1,200 lb @ $1.20)	1,440	
	2,940	
Purchases: Resin (2,000 lb @ $3.00)	6,000	
Cement (6,000 lb @ $1.20)	7,200	
Total Raw Material Available	16,140	
Less Ending Raw Material Inventory		
Resin (500 lb @ $3.00)	1,500	
Cement (1,200 lb @ $1.20)	1,440	
Raw Materials Used	13,200	
Direct Labor (2 hr @ $15/hr × 2,000 gnomes)	60,000	
Mfg. Overhead:		
Variable (0.30 × $60,000)	18,000	
Fixed	15,000	
Cost of Goods Manufactured		106,200
Cost of Goods Available for Sale		116,820
Less Ending Finished Goods Inventory (200 @ $53.10)		10,620
Cost of Goods Sold		106,200
Gross Profit		93,800
Less Marketing and Administrative Expenses		
Variable (0.10 × $200,000)	20,000	
Fixed	50,000	70,000
Operating Income		$23,800

Figure 7.1

what caused the variances for labor, materials and variable overhead? Let's peel down another layer and analyze these variances a bit more closely.

The level of analysis in Figure 7.4 introduces the flexible budget. A flexible budget can be thought of as an after-the-fact budget which

The Riley Company
Income – 2012

Sales (2,100 gnomes)		$208,000
Less Cost of Goods Sold:		
Beginning Finished Goods Inventory (200 @ $53.10)		$10,620
Beginning Raw Materials Inventories		
Resin (500 lb @ $3.00)	$1,500	
Cement (1,200 lb @ $1.20)	1,440	
	2,940	
Purchases: Resin (2,000 lb)	6,100	
Cement (6,000 lb)	7,250	
Total Raw Material Available	16,290	
Less Ending Raw Material Inventory		
Resin (310 lb @ $3.00)	930	
Cement (900 lb @ $1.20)	1,080	
Raw Materials Used	14,280	
Direct Labor (4,500 hours)	66,375	
Mfg. Overhead:		
Variable (0.30 × $63,000)	18,900	
Fixed	15,000	
Cost of Goods Manufactured	114,555	
Cost of Goods Available for Sale	125,175	
Less Ending Finished Goods Inventory (150 @ $53.10)	7,965	
Cost of Goods Sold		117,210
Gross Profit		90,790
Less Marketing and Administrative Expenses		
Variable (0.10 × $230,000)	23,000	
Fixed	49,000	
		72,000
Operating Income		$18,790

Figure 7.2

we can use for control purposes. As we mentioned earlier, it is based on the actual level of sales and production and the standard, or budgeted, per-unit sales price and costs. In other words it shows us what revenues and costs should have been at the actual level of sales

The Riley Company
Comparison of Budgeted and Actual Income Statement Items

	Budget	Actual	Difference
Unit Sales	2,000	2,100	100
Sales	$200,000	$208,000	$8,000
Less Cost of Goods Sold:			
Beginning Finished Goods Inventory	10,620	10,620	–0–
Beginning Raw Materials Inventories			
Resin (500 lb @ $3.00)	1,500	1,500	–0–
Cement (1,200 lb @ $1.20)	1,440	1,440	–0–
Total Beg. Materials Inv.	2,940	2,940	–0–
Purchases: Resin	6,000	6,100	(100)
Cement	7,200	7,250	(50)
Total Raw Material Available	16,140	16,290	(150)
Less Ending Raw Material Inventory			
Resin (310 lb @ $3.00)	1,500	930	(570)
Cement (900 lb @ $1.20)	1,440	1,080	(360)
Raw Materials Used	13,200	14,280	(1,080)
Direct Labor	60,000	66,375	(6,375)
Mfg. Overhead:			
Variable	18,000	18,900	(900)
Fixed	15,000	15,000	–0–
Cost of Goods Manufactured	106,200	114,555	(8,355)
Cost of Goods Available for Sale	116,820	125,175	(8,355)
Less Ending Fin. Goods Inv.	10,620	7,965	(2,655)
Cost of Goods Sold	106,200	117,210	(11,010)
Gross Profit	93,800	90,790	(3,010)
Less Marketing and Administrative Expenses			
Variable (0.10 × $200,000)	20,000	23,000	(3,000)
Fixed	50,000	49,000	1,000
Operating Income	$23,800	$18,790	($5,010)

Figure 7.3

if actual revenues and costs per unit had met our original budget projections. In the above example, the flexible budget revenue is $210,000. That was calculated on the actual units sold (2,100) and

	Actual	Flexible Budget Variance	Flexible Budget	Sales Volume Variance	Static Budget
The Riley Company					
Comparison of Actual Results to Flexible and Static Budgets					
Unit Sales	2,100		2,100	1,000 (F)	2,000
Revenue	$208,000	$2,000(U)	$210,000	$10,000(F)	$200,000
Variable Costs					
Direct Materials:					
Resin	6,670	370(U)	6,300	300(U)	6,000
Cement	7,610	50(U)	7,560	360(U)	7,200
Direct Labor	66,375	3,375(U)	63,000	3,000(U)	60,000
Variable Mfg. Overhead	18,900	0	18,900	900(U)	18,000
Var. Mkt. & Admin.	23,000	2,000(U)	21,000	1,000(U)	20,000
Contrib. Margin	$85,445	$7,495(U)	$93,240	4,440(F)	88,800
Fixed Costs:					
Fixed Mfg. Overhead	15,000	0	15,000	0	15,000
Fixed Mkg. & Admin.	49,000	1,000(F)	50,000	0	50,000
Plus End F.G. Inv.	7,965	2,655(U)	10,620		10,620
Less Beg. F.G. Inv.	10,620		10,620		10,620
Operating Income	$18,790	$9,150(U)	$27,940	$4,400(F)	$23,800

F = favorable; U = unfavorable

Figure 7.4

the budgeted sales price per unit ($100). Likewise, the amount shown on the flexible budget for labor is $63,000, calculated as $15 per hour times two hours ($30) per gnome for 2,100 gnomes. The same approach is used for direct materials.

The level of analysis in Figure 7.3 merely showed that our actual sales were $8,000 greater than our budget. We can now see that that was the result of two offsetting factors. We actually sold 1,000 more units than anticipated, which resulted in a favorable sales volume variance of $10,000, but we sold these units for less than budgeted, which results in an unfavorable price variance of $2,000.

As we move down the columns of the chart we see that our direct materials variances were largely due to the fact that we used more material because we made more units than budgeted for. Likewise, $3,000 of the direct labor variance of $6,375 was due to the fact that we made more units than we budgeted for.

As an aside, we should point out that these so-called unfavorable volume variances aren't really unfavorable. They are generally referred to as unfavorable because they explain in part why actual amounts are more than budgeted, but they arise simply because we made and sold more units than budgeted, which is a good thing.

We have now looked at several different levels of analysis and definitely have a better idea of areas we need to look at in order to control costs than we did when we merely compared the budget with the actual income statement. We can, however, go to a yet deeper level of analysis. We can peel off another layer of the onion.

Look at the flexible budget variance column in Figure 7.4. Are these variances due to the fact that we used more materials and labor per gnome than was budgeted or because we paid a higher price for the materials and a higher wage for labor than we budgeted? How about the zero variance for variable overhead? Does this indicate that we have everything under control, or is it possible that we have two offsetting variances? Our analysis to date does not give us an answer to these questions. It's time to start peeling.

Since a firm will often purchase either more or less materials than they use during any given period of time, we need to separate the amount purchased from the amount used. Figure 7.5 indicates how this is done. In the Riley Company's case, it purchased 2,000 pounds of resin at $3.05 per pound while the budgeted price was $3.00. This resulted in a $100 unfavorable price variance. The usage variance is based on the difference between how much it used and what the budgeted amount called for at the actual level of production. In this case, Riley used 90 pounds more than was budgeted. For cement it paid a bit more than budgeted, but it used the same amount that was called for in the budget.

Calculating labor wage rate and efficiency variances is similar to that for material variances, but a bit simpler because labor cannot

The Riley Company
Analysis of Flexible Budget Variances
Direct Materials Variances

	Actual	Purchased Price Variance	Std. Price × Act. Quant.	Used Std. Price × Act. Quant.	Usage Variance	Flexible Budget
Resin	2,000 lb × $3.05		2,000 lb × $3.00	2,190 lb × $3.00		2,100 lb × $1 × $3.00
	$6,100	$100(U)	$6,000	$6,570	$270(U)	$6,300
Cement	6,000 lb × $1.2084		6,000 lb × $1.20	6,300 lb × $1.20		2,100 lb × $3 × $1.20
	$7,250	$50(U)	$7,200	$7,560	$0	$7,560

Direct Labor Variances

	Actual	Wage Rate Variance	Std. Price × Act. Quant.	Efficiency Variance	Flexible Budget
	4,500 hrs × $14.75		4,500 hrs × $15.00		2,100 × 2 hrs × $15.00
	$66,375	$1,125(F)	$67,500	$4,500(U)	$63,000

F = favorable; U = unfavorable

Figure 7.5

be "inventoried" in the same sense that raw materials and finished goods can. In examining the Riley Company's data we find that they paid a lower wage than was budgeted, but had an unfavorable efficiency variance. Could there perhaps be a cause and effect relationship between the favorable wage rate variance and the unfavorable labor efficiency variance?

Actual variable overhead costs for the Riley Company were exactly the same as the flexible budget called for. Without this level of analysis, one would assume that the Riley Company had their variable overhead costs in perfect order. As Figure 7.6 indicates, however, that was not the case at all. It just so happened that two large variances, one favorable and one unfavorable, offset each other. It's worth noting

The Riley Company
Analysis of Variable Overhead Variances

Actual Var. Overhead	Spending Variance	Actual Input Quantity × Rate	Efficiency Variance	Flexible Budget
		$66,375 × 0.30		2 hr × 2,100 × $15 × 0.30
$18,900	$1,012.50(F)	$19,912.50	$1,012.50(U)	$18,900.00

F = favorable; U = unfavorable

Figure 7.6

that the variable overhead efficiency variance measures the efficiency of the activity on which overhead is allocated. In the Riley Company's case they allocated overhead costs to their products on the basis of labor. So once again we see that labor was not used efficiently.

Variances are a bit like the red light on the dashboard of your car. They don't tell you exactly what is wrong, but they do notify you when things are not working as they should. When you're driving down the freeway at 70 miles per hour and the red light on your dashboard comes on, it is saying, "You might want to think about slowing down and taking this car into the mechanic and letting him figure out what is wrong before you destroy your engine." A large unfavorable variance tells you the same sort of thing about your organization. It's telling you that your operations might be out of control and you should investigate. Furthermore, the level of analysis presented in Figures 7.5 and 7.6 will tell us where to look.

Flexible budgets and variance analysis permit management by exception. When you compare standard and actual costs and then analyze variances between the two, you place yourself in a position to focus attention and efforts on areas that are not operating as they should. You can then spend less time on areas identified as operating within expectations.

Not all variances, however, need to be investigated. The market prices of many commodities are in a constant state of flux. Likewise, the price of raw materials a company uses in its production of goods often fluctuates both up and down over time. Small price variances reflect these random fluctuations. Also, there are often a number of factors that have a small, temporary effect on usage and efficiency variances. If we examine the Riley Company's material variances we don't see anything particularly worrisome.

On the other hand, large variances could indicate that the production system is out of control or there has been a systemic change in the firm's operating environment. When this is the case, the cause of such variances needs to be explored. The longer your production system is out of order, the more money you are going to lose.

In the normal course of business a firm's accounting system might generate many variances. This raises the question as to which variances should be investigated. Variance investigation can be costly and time consuming. In most cases, managers do not have the time to run down every variance that gets reported, and it is probably not necessary that they do. While there are sophisticated mathematical models for determining which variances should be investigated, the decision to investigate or not is often subjective or made on a rule-of-thumb basis. A commonsense approach would suggest that you investigate large variances you can do something about.

When investigating variances it is a good idea to keep in mind that they are often interrelated. For example, suppose that the purchasing department has an opportunity to purchase materials at a "bargain" price. We've all probably bought something at a so-called bargain price only to find out later that it was of inferior quality. If the firm puts these bargain-priced materials into production they might quickly find that they were no bargain at all and wind up with unfavorable material and labor efficiency variances. It may not always be true that you get what you pay for, but it is always true that you pay for what you get.

Summary

A flexible budget is useful for control purposes, whereas master budgets as presented in the previous chapter are prepared for planning purposes. Flexible budgets are built on standard variable costs per unit and separate variable from fixed costs. As production and sales increase or decrease, variable costs and revenues should keep pace, thereby allowing managers to better compare actual with budgeted performance. For control purposes, then, flexible budgets are more informative than static budgets.

This chapter demonstrates how price and efficiency variances are calculated and presents four different levels of analysis. Variances do not necessarily tell managers why actual results are different than budgeted, but they do alert managers that there is a difference and give them an idea as to where to look to find the cause of the difference.

Exercises

1   In what ways is a flexible budget analysis more informative than a static budget analysis?
2   Why do companies use standard costs? How can variance analysis and standard costs aid in a program of continuous improvement?
3   List examples of where a favorable variance might lead to unfavorable variances in other areas.
4   Kruger and Huff Enterprises manufacture and sell wooden statues of biblical figures. Their budget for the coming year calls for sales of 10,000 units at $200 per unit; 30,000 board feet of 18 × 18 wood beams at $10 per foot; 40,000 hours of direct labor at $15 per hour; and $600,000 of variable overhead costs. In addition, the budget called for sales and administrative expenses of $250,000. Variable overhead was to be assigned to the products on the basis of labor costs at a rate of $1 of overhead for every dollar of labor. Fixed overhead budgeted at $100,000.

Actual sales were 10,500 units for $2,050,000. They purchased 32,000 feet of beams for $339,063 and used 32,000 feet. Their actual labor costs were $625,000 for 41,500 hours; variable overhead, $620,000; fixed overhead, $125,000; and selling and administration, $240,000.

(a) Prepare a static budget.
(b) Prepare a flexible budget.
(c) Calculate all possible variances.
(d) Comment on the variances, and postulate possible reasons for them.

8

ALLOCATION

Chapter Overview

This chapter discusses why allocations in accounting are unavoidable and how they render the numbers on accounting statements somewhat arbitrary. After studying this chapter you will:

- Understand the arbitrary nature of all allocation schemes and the impact allocation has on accounting numbers;
- Know why accounting allocations are both necessary and inescapable;
- Know the different approaches to allocation;
- Understand that different allocation methods result in different costs charged to various products;
- Realize that broad-based allocation methods hide the cause of product and service costs;
- Understand the basic differences between traditional and activity-based cost accounting systems.

* * * * *

Allocations are, by their very nature, arbitrary, which means that whatever is being allocated could be allocated differently. That is to say, allocations and their resulting numbers are contingent solely upon one's discretion. Different persons might make equally valid allocations in an entirely different manner.

Here is an example. Each of us is constantly allocating our time and money to competing opportunities. Some folks allocate four hours a day to watching television; some allocate four hours a day to studying the classics; some spend four hours a day volunteering at the local shelter; and so on. Who is to say that one course of action is better than another or that there is not yet another way to allocate one's time that would bring even more benefit to the individual?

There is no single "correct" way to allocate. There are, however, more useful ways. About all we can say is that different allocation methods bring about different results. Depending on our goals, we can say that one method may bring us closer to our goal than others. If our goal is to become a soap-opera critic, watching television for four hours a day will probably bring us closer to that goal than helping down at the soup kitchen.

Many of the costs an organization incurs relate to two or more products, services, departments or periods of time. These are what we call common costs, because they are common to two or more cost objects. *Kohler's Dictionary for Accountants* (6th ed.) defines allocation as "The process of charging an item or group of items of revenue or cost to one or more objects, activities, processes, operations or products . . ."

A perfect example is the cost of a building that houses a firm's production, marketing and administrative activities. Since the building has a life of, say, 40 to 50 years, we need first to determine how much of the total cost of the building should be allocated to each year. We can depreciate the building over a period anywhere from 40 to 50 years. Next we determine how much of each year's depreciation expense to allocate to each department. If the organization produces two or more products, we then need to determine how much of the production department's share of the building should be charged to each of the different products. At this point we are allocating previously allocated costs. The cost of each product now contains costs that have been allocated three times: first to a time period, then to a department and finally to the product. And each of these allocations is arbitrary. We could provide many more examples, but you get the picture. So put aside any notions you had about accounting numbers being precise.

FASB and the SEC have issued hundreds of pronouncements over the years. Some of these dicta deal with the format and presentation of accounting data, some merely clarify earlier pronouncements and some deal with various procedures. The vast bulk of them, however, deal with the allocation problem. It is an important problem. It is *the* accounting problem. There is no escaping it either. As long as there are costs common to two or more cost objects we must allocate.

Necessity of Allocations

Accounting is useful for many different purposes, and there are just as many different reasons why it is necessary that we allocate costs. Some of these are:

1 **To determine the cost of products or services.** While allocating common overhead costs to individual products and services cannot give us the *true* cost of any individual item, recognizing the cost across all products will give us a good idea of the total cost of production. For example, if we manufacture chairs and tables, we will never know how much of our insurance premium is in the cost of either chairs or tables. We will, however, know the total cost of insurance spread across our total production.

2 **To encourage intelligent use of common resources.** When the cost of common assets is allocated to department budgets on a usage basis, department managers tend to monitor the use of these resources more closely.

3 **To aid in decision making.** Making decisions on the basis of allocated costs is a risky business. As we shall subsequently see, allocated costs can be very misleading, and misleading data is worse than no data. However, having said this, allocated costs can be useful in giving managers an idea of the total costs involved. If we allocate maintenance costs to the assembly department, the manager of that department becomes more cognizant of these costs and will presumably take action to use maintenance department services wisely.

Approaches to Allocation

While allocation is arbitrary, there are some approaches that will produce better results than others.

1   If there is a **causal relationship** between the cost and some factor, use that factor when allocating costs. An example of this might be the cost of xeroxing. If we can measure the number of copies different departments make, it is a simple matter to charge each department on the basis of usage. This is without a doubt the preferred approach. The only problem is that there is not always a causal relationship between the cost and the cost object.

2   Another approach is to allocate on the basis of **relative benefits received**. The problem here is that it is difficult to measure benefits. Consider this example: A department store is trying to measure the profitability of its different departments and has decided it needs to allocate the lease payments on the building to the various departments. The store's accountant suggests allocating on the basis of square feet occupied by each department. The manager of the jewelry department thinks that is a great idea. The manager of the furniture department thinks it is a terrible idea. Why? The obvious reason is that sofas and tables require more space than earrings and bracelets. Furthermore, the furniture department is probably on the fourth floor where customers go only if they want to buy furniture, and the jewelry department is going to be in a high-traffic area and will attract impulse shoppers. One more factor is that the markup for jewelry is usually significantly higher than for furniture.

3   **Fairness and equity** seem like a good way to allocate. After all, don't all reasonable people want to be fair and equitable? The obvious problem here, of course, is what is fair and equitable to you might not be fair and equitable to the next person. Fairness, like beauty, is often in the eye of the beholder.

4   Allocating costs between segments of an organization on the
     basis of their respective **ability to bear** is not infrequently used.
     Generally speaking, it is not a good method to use. Consider
     this example: You and I are division managers for Megacorp.
     Our divisions are generally of the same size and profitability.
     This coming year you work very hard and increase your sales
     20 percent. I slack off, play a lot of golf and go fishing. As a
     result my division's sales decrease 20 percent. (I blame it on the
     regional economy.) The company allocates advertising expense
     to the different divisions on the basis of sales dollars. What hap-
     pens here? Your reward for working harder is to pick up more
     advertising expense. I will be allocated less. You have, in a sense,
     helped subsidize my division. Thank you very much.

Allocating Overhead

There are three components of cost to any manufactured product:
direct labor, direct materials and overhead. This is true whether we
are speaking of the manufacture of something as simple as a coffee
cup or as complicated as a Boeing 747. In a service-industry organization, there are generally only two cost components – direct labor
and overhead.

Direct labor and direct material costs can be traced directly to
individual products. If we are producing chairs and desks, we can
trace the cost of wood directly to each individual chair and each individual desk. The same is true with direct labor. If it takes two hours to
make a chair and we pay our workers $15 an hour, we know that the
cost of direct labor going into each chair is, on average, $30. Like-
wise, we can determine the cost of labor going into each desk. Overhead costs, however, are common across all products. Costs such as
depreciation of factory equipment, plant utilities, insurance, maintenance, supervision and other indirect manufacturing costs are very
definitely costs of production. We couldn't make products without
incurring them. Allocating these overhead costs to individual products is the single largest cost accounting issue for both manufacturing
and service companies.

This raises the question of how much rent, insurance and these other overhead costs are in that chair we produced. If we also make desks, how much overhead should be allocated to chairs and how much to desks? The short answer is we will have to use some arbitrary method to allocate these costs to the chairs, tables, sofas and whatever else it is that we might be producing. This is also true in service industries when we need to calculate the cost of services provided for different clients.

With the recent advances in production technology, overhead has become a far more important element in the total cost of many products and services. In high-tech industries it is not uncommon to find total product costs consisting of 60 to 70 percent overhead. If we misallocate overhead, products and service costs will become either over- or understated. We won't have the information we need to make intelligent marketing and production decisions.

Let's assume we manufacture two products in the same factory. If we allocate too much overhead to product A it will appear to cost more than it really does. If we base sales prices on a cost basis we are likely to overprice product A and will likely lose sales to our competitors. And because the amount of overhead is finite, we would, in turn, allocate less to product B. Under-allocating overhead to product B we would likely price it at an amount that provides for a low profit margin or, worse, at a price that does not cover our true costs. In this case product A is subsidizing product B. In a competitive environment both of those scenarios are bad. It is important that our accounting system capture and report the true economics of our production process.

Traditional Overhead Accounting

Traditionally, overhead has been allocated to products and services by lumping all the overhead accounts into a single cost pool and then dividing total overhead costs by some measure of activity such as direct labor hours or machine hours. The resulting figure is known as the overhead application rate. To illustrate, assume we use number of hours machinery is operated as our measure of activity and overhead costs are as follows:

Factory rent	$500,000
Setup costs	100,000
Insurance	50,000
Maintenance	60,000
Utilities	20,000
Small tools	15,000
Indirect labor	25,000
Miscellaneous	20,000
Supervision	80,000
Total overhead	$870,000
Estimated machine hours	125,000

Our overhead application rate becomes $6.96 per machine hour ($870,000 ÷ 125,000).

If we manufacture a batch of 100 chairs and use 500 machine hours we will allocate $3,480 (500 hours × $6.96 per hour) to that batch or $34.80 per chair.

One of the problems with this approach is that it assumes all overhead costs increase proportionately with production volume. In our example, if machine hours increase 10 percent for the next batch of chairs, we will allocate 10 percent more overhead costs to that batch. But the reality is that some of those overhead costs are fixed and will not increase. Some overhead items might increase more than 10 percent. Some might increase less than 10 percent. Factors other than production volume drive many manufacturing overhead costs.

The traditional approach to overhead allocation has been referred to as the peanut butter approach. As with peanut butter we dip our knife (application rate) into the jar (single cost pool) and spread overhead across all our products. Let's assume for the moment that $34.80 per chair is a reasonable number. (For marketing decisions that's the best we can hope for.) Being good managers we want to control overhead costs. What information does the traditional method provide to help us control them? Absolutely none. What caused maintenance to be $60,000 or small tools to cost $15,000? Our accounting system doesn't provide us with so much as a clue. Yet a competitive market requires a firm to have a good handle on its costs. In order to control costs we not only have to know how much they are, but we also have to know what caused them.

If you don't know what your product or service really costs, and if you don't know what causes those costs, you're not going to be in a position to control them and consequently you're not likely to be in business for very long.

The whole purpose behind management accounting is to provide useful information to management for planning, organizing, controlling, directing and decision making. Knowing this raises the question, "How do you know if your accounting system is providing you with useful information or not?" You cannot take it as a matter of faith that it is. We have previously illustrated the point that misleading information is worse than no information.

The business world is dynamic, ever changing, constantly adapting to new technologies and global competition. We all know the fate of companies that were unable or unwilling to change. Their names can be found in dusty history books, but not on today's products and services.

Both internal and external forces combine to constantly create new challenges for management. If accounting systems are to provide useful information, they must be able to react quickly to changes in the environment. As production systems become more sophisticated and complex, management must see to it that accounting systems capture the economics of the new technology.

If an accounting system cannot provide the information management needs to meet new challenges, it stands the risk of becoming obsolete and will inevitably provide information that is either incomplete or inaccurate. Relying on such information will lead you into making dysfunctional or less than optimal decisions. If you know where to look, however, you can find symptoms of bad information. You need to check for them periodically.

In a *Harvard Business Review* article ("You Need a New Cost System When . . .", *Harvard Business Review*, Jan.–Feb., 1989), Robin Cooper pointed to signs indicating that your cost system might be giving you bad information. Here is what he said to look for:

1   What do production personnel say about different products? Are some products more difficult to produce than others? If so, does your accounting system reflect that? If not, the way it allocates overhead could be hiding inefficiencies. Allocating overhead to different products is inherently problematic. Closely examine how your system allocates overhead. Does it reflect the additional costs involved in producing these difficult-to-produce products?

Here is an example where a firm's overhead allocation system provided worse than poor information: A Wichita, Kansas based manufacturing firm makes two related items: two-wheeled hand trucks and four-wheeled garden wagons. The firm's accountant allocated overhead evenly between the two products on a per-unit basis. The hand trucks, however, required six welds, while the wagons required ten. On average the wagons took 50 percent longer to manufacture than the hand trucks. Consequently the firm did not have any idea of the overhead associated with the different products. The accountant's "peanut butter" approach to allocating overhead resulted in the hand trucks being over-costed and the wagons under-costed. In essence the hand trucks were subsidizing the wagons. Furthermore, the system provided management with no information for controlling costs.

2   What do marketing managers say about different products? Are your products being priced competitively? Are profit margins of some of your products hard to explain? If you have products that show great profit margins and no one else is in the market, you need to be asking why. Could it be that you are simply under-costing your product and not really making the profit you think you are?

3   Or could the obverse be true? Do competitors' prices seem unreasonably low? Perhaps your cost of making the product is higher than the price at which your competitor is selling it. Is this because the competitor is just far more efficient, or does it have a different cost structure? Or is your cost system not accurately reflecting true costs? Before adjustments in accounting

for overhead were made, the Wichita firm was trying (unsuc-
cessfully) to justify higher prices for hand trucks and probably
losing sales and market share.

4   How have technology and competition affected your produc-
    tion process? Have you made significant changes? Have you
    changed the way you allocate overhead costs? If you have
    automated production and are still allocating costs on the basis
    of direct labor, you are probably not capturing the true costs
    of production. Accounting systems are supposed to reflect eco-
    nomic reality. To do so, they need to capture the economics of
    the production process.

5   Has there been a change in the firm's product mix? Is the
    firm producing new products that require a different mix of
    resources than has been used in the past? Do the new products
    require more or less overhead in proportion to direct labor
    than products produced in the past?

Activity-Based Costing (ABC)

ABC is an alternative method of overhead allocation which provides
managers with better information for making decisions and controlling costs. It seeks to measure the cost of the different activities that go
into the production of products and services. It is based on the notion
that the production of goods and services requires activities and that
activities consume resources which cost money.

ABC requires a real hands-on approach by the firm's accountants.
The first step in implementing an ABC system is to identify the major
activities that take place in a production system. This is true whether
you are producing a product or a service. It's as true for a hospital, a
school or a church as it is for a steel mill.

Instead of sitting in their corner office, accountants need to get
out and about in the factory, the reception area and others' offices to
visit with and gain insight from front-line supervisors, service personnel, assembly-line workers, secretaries, maintenance people, supply
clerks and janitors – everyone, that is, who is involved in any sort of
production-related activity.

After identifying the production activities taking place, the next step is to determine whether these activities add value to the product or not. How can we tell if an activity adds value to a product or service? If the customer is willing to pay for the results of that activity, it adds value. If not, it doesn't. If you buy a new car, you pay more because it is painted. Painting is an activity which you were willing to pay for; hence it adds value. The factory where that car was assembled has a parts inventory. Managing inventory, storing it, moving it, insuring it, securing it and so on involve activities which can be quite costly. If that inventory is overly large it imposes extra costs that, as a customer, you're probably not interested in paying for.

Here is where ABC makes a positive – and perhaps its most fundamental – contribution, before a single number is entered into a ledger. By going into service providers' offices, the inventory store room or the factory floor and identifying value-adding and non-value-adding activities, the company is now in a position to eliminate the non-value-adding activities and seek ways to perform the value-adding activities more efficiently. Activities are like weeds. If they are not monitored, they will continue to grow and choke off profitability.

Take a close look at the activities within the unit of your organization with which you are most familiar. Ask people why they perform various activities. You will get answers like "That's the way they taught me" or "I don't know; we've just always done it that way." By taking the time and effort to look closely at the activities that take place and determining if they add value you'll be surprised – and be able to save money.

The second step in developing an ABC system is to determine the cost of the various activities and group them into cost pools, with a different cost pool for each activity. A cost pool is nothing more than a grouping of individual costs. For example, equipment maintenance is a common activity and can be considered a cost pool. What costs are involved? Obviously, this will vary from firm to firm, but generally speaking maintenance costs include wages, small tools, supplies and down time.

Setups, inventory management, quality control, security and front-line supervision are examples of other overhead-incurring activities that one might find in a factory. Likewise, a bank may identify primary activities of processing customer deposits and withdrawals, processing loans, preparing monthly statements and reconciling cash drawers.

Once activities and their costs have been identified, our next step is to determine what principal factor drives those costs. This may not be readily apparent, and what appears to be the cause may not be. For example, what is it that drives total setup costs? A possible answer might be the number of setups, which are determined by the size of the batches produced, which, in turn, are determined by the size of the orders our sales department makes.

The final step is to allocate these costs to the product, using the cost drivers as the basis of allocation.

ABC has obvious advantages over the more traditional approach to overhead allocation:

1   ABC identifies the activities, both value-adding and non-value-adding, that cause overhead costs.
2   ABC identifies the driver of those costs, thereby giving us the means of control and performance evaluation.
3   ABC reduces the number of times a cost is allocated and provides a causal relationship between the cost and the cost object.
4   ABC better captures the economics of the production process, thereby providing relevant information for decision making that traditional costing does not.

* * * * *

Let's compare the two methods.

Trekker Corporation manufacture high-end mountain bikes and touring bikes. They currently allocate overhead costs on the basis of direct labor hours. Last month they manufactured 1,000 mountain bikes and 800 touring bikes. They used 5,000 labor hours to produce

Activity	Cost	Cost Driver	Activity Level Mountain	Touring	Overhead/ Unit of Cost Driver
Inventory handling	$50,000	Number of components	45	55	$500
Setups	80,000	Number of setups	20	30	1,600
Machining	70,000	Machine hours	50	90	500
Quality control	40,000	Number of inspections	15	25	1,000
Total overhead costs	$240,000				

Required: Calculate the overhead costs assigned to mountain and touring bikes using traditional overhead costing based on labor hours and ABC using cost drivers.

Solution: In using the traditional approach we divide total overhead by the allocation base of direct labor and then allocate overhead to the products on the basis of direct labor hours used. In this case, $240,000 ÷ 11,000 hours = $21.82 per direct labor hour. For mountain bikes we allocate $109,100 ($21.82 × 5,000 hours). This amounts to $109.10 overhead per bike. We will allocate $130,920 ($21.82 × 6,000 hours) or $163.65 of overhead to each touring bike.

This is the peanut butter approach. We have used a broad knife to spread the overhead across both products. Consequently, we don't know what caused overhead costs to be what they are, nor do we know if the amount we allocated to each product is reasonable. These numbers give us no insight or information for making pricing or production decisions. In short, we have not captured the economics of producing bicycles.

Figure 8.1

mountain bikes and 6,000 hours to produce touring bikes. They are considering using ABC in the future. Consider the data in Figure 8.1.

Using ABC we get the following overhead costs charged to our two products:

	Mountain	Touring	Total
Inventory handling	$22,500	$27,500	$50,000
Setups	32,000	48,000	80,000
Machining	25,000	45,000	70,000
Quality control	15,000	25,000	40,000
Total allocated	$ 94,500	$145,500	$240,000

On a per unit basis we now have $94,500 \div 1,000 = 94.50 for mountain bikes and $145,500 \div 800 = 181.88 for touring bikes.

Trekker Corporation now have a better handle on the economics of their production process. They know what the activities are that caused their overhead costs and consequently they are now better able to control them. They also have a more accurate picture of the true costs of each line of bicycle.

In traditional costing, cost centers are usually departments and other organizational units. For example, the production, maintenance and marketing departments, the downtown store, the uptown store, and the West Coast and East Coast divisions are where costs are accumulated. The advantage of this system is that it provides a way to trace costs to the managers of these units who are responsible for controlling costs. The disadvantage is that many of the costs over which the managers have no control are often allocated to the departments.

In ABC, activities become the cost centers. Activities often cross over departmental and product lines. The advantage here is that it is the activities themselves that cause the costs to be incurred. If we can control the activity, we can control the cost.

In traditional costing, a cost pool may contain many different costs that have little or no relation to one another. For example, overhead for the assembly department may include depreciation, maintenance, insurance and supervision along with other costs. Some of these will be variable; some will be fixed. Some will be historical (depreciation); some will be current (maintenance). Some will be incurred directly by the department (supervision); some will be allocated (insurance). On the other hand, in ABC, cost pools tend to be more homogeneous. The costs will relate directly to a specific activity.

In traditional costing, the total cost of a product consists of direct materials, direct labor and overhead costs allocated from different production departments. For example, it might consist of overhead costs allocated from the sub-assembly department, the assembly department and the finishing department. Remember, some of these costs were allocated to the departments in the first place; hence we have costs arbitrarily allocated twice before they reach the product.

In ABC, the total cost of a product consists of direct materials, direct labor and the cost of the production activities. Consequently in a system which uses ABC, there are fewer allocated costs and more costs which can be traced directly to the product. Costs become less arbitrary and more direct.

The basic objectives of the two systems are different. The basic objective of traditional systems is to provide data for external financial reporting. If you are an investor, potential creditor or government agency, you are not particularly concerned with the cost of specific activities of the production process. You are more interested in the "big picture." You want to know what the total assets and the firm's profits are. Traditional accounting serves this purpose well. The basic objective of ABC is to provide data for internal reporting, cost control, managerial decision making and performance evaluation.

At this point you may be thinking, "ABC sounds great. Why don't more organizations use it?" There are two basic reasons: costs and familiarity. ABC systems cost more than traditional because they require more measuring and closer monitoring. While they do provide better information, they are labor intensive.

Traditional cost systems have been around in one form or another since the early twentieth century, when direct labor, not overhead, constituted the largest component of product costs. They are relatively simple to construct and inexpensive to implement. Furthermore, managers are familiar and often comfortable with traditional systems. Put yourself in the place of the production manager of a firm when a consultant suggests the firm adopt a new system for determining costs. The manager probably understands the current system and has had his or her performance evaluated on the basis of this system. He or she may well see the new system as a threat. It is not unlike the athlete who is winning the game and the referee says, "Let's change the way we keep score." To be successful, the consultant will need to educate the manager to the long-term benefits of ABC and help the manager realize that he or she will be more efficient by having more relevant data available.

Differences between Traditional and ABC Allocations

We can summarize the basic differences between traditional and ABC overhead allocation systems as follows:

Table 8.1

Item		Traditional Costing	Activity-Based Costing
1	Cost centers	Departments	Activities
2	Cost pools	Diverse costs	Costs more homogeneous
3	Allocation bases	Few	Many – related to different activities
4	Variable costs	Assumed to vary with number of units produced	Vary with number of units, batches and different products
5	Product costs	Direct materials, direct labor and overhead allocated from different departments	Direct materials, direct labor and cost of production activities
6	Use of non-financial measures	Few	Many
7	(Non-)value-adding measures	Not identified	Identified
8	Complexity of manufacturing process	Not captured	Captured
9	Basic objectives	Inventory valuation and external financial reporting	Cost reduction, managerial decision making and performance evaluation

Summary

It is widely acknowledged that allocation is one of the most intractable problems facing accountants. This chapter discusses various allocation methods and points out that allocations by their nature are arbitrary, thus introducing an element of arbitrariness into the accounting process. For management purposes, "correctness" of allocations is not necessarily germane. The main issue is usefulness. Are allocations made in such a way as to provide managers with the information they need for effective planning, controlling and decision making?

One of the most useful recent developments in managerial accounting has been the introduction of activity-based accounting (ABC),which provides a way to allocate costs that provides information more useful for controlling costs and implementing total quality improvement programs.

The principal difference between ABC and traditional cost accounting systems lies in the fact that ABC allocates costs to activities, whereas traditional costing allocates costs to departments or units within an organization. This chapter illustrates an ABC system and lists nine major differences between ABC and traditional systems.

Exercises

1   House of the Sun Foods processes and sells organic, vegan foods to health food stores and the public in Seattle, Washington. It is considering switching from a traditional costing system to an activity-based costing system to determine costs of its various products. It currently allocates overhead on the basis of direct labor hours. During the past quarter it produced, among other products, 6,000 baskets containing a four-course dinner for a party of six and 2,000 dessert packages containing eight separate dessert items. Its direct materials costs were $36,000 for the dinner baskets and $8,000 for the dessert packages. House of the Sun Foods' direct labor costs are $18 per hour. It can produce, on average, four baskets and two dessert packages per direct labor hour. A total of 2,500 direct labor hours were worked.

After a thorough study, the controller for House of the Sun Foods concluded the following:

Activity	Dinner Baskets	Dessert Packages	Total
Material handling	6,000 units	2,000 units	8,000 units
Dehydrating	4,000 hours	2,000 hours	6,000 hours
Assembly	3,000 inspections	3,000 inspections	6,000 inspections
Testing	4,000 tests	2,000 tests	6,000 tests

Additionally, the following overhead cost information is available for the quarter. Management plans on producing and selling 8,000 baskets next quarter.

Activity	Cost	Cost Driver	Allocation Rate
Material handling	$16,000	Number of units	$2.00 per basket
Dehydrating	12,000	Number of hrs	2.00 per hour
Assembly	3,000	Number of inspections	0.50 per inspection
Testing	12,000	Number of tests	2.00 per test
Total overhead	$43,000		

Required: Estimate the unit product costs for dinner baskets and dessert packages for next quarter using the traditional and ABC approaches.

2   What consequences can the "peanut butter" approach have on product costs?

3   What are the consequences of over- or under-costing products?

4   List four uses House of the Sun Foods' managers might make of
    ABC costing.

5   What are some signs that might indicate House of the Sun Foods'
    traditional cost accounting system is not providing its manage-
    ment with the information they need?

9

FINANCIAL STATEMENT ANALYSIS

Chapter Overview

This chapter is about reading, analyzing and understanding the information contained in an organization's financial statements. After reading this chapter you will:

- Be better able to read and understand financial statements
- Be able to compare different firms' financial information
- Gain new insights into firms' operations and financial health
- Understand the concepts of liquidity, leverage, asset activity and profitability

* * * * *

Financial statements reveal a lot more about a company than what it earned, what it owes and the historical value of its assets. To bring the economics of a firm into focus you need to study and thoroughly analyze its financial statements. That's what this chapter is about.

It is important to realize that no individual figures on a financial statement are very useful in and of themselves. You might, from time to time, hear (or even have said) something like, "You don't need to throw all those numbers at me. I'm only interested in the bottom line."

Let's go straight to that bottom line. Two bottom lines in fact: Company A and Company B. Let's say that Company A's income statement reveals a net income of $50,000 and Company B a net income of $100,000. Company B made twice the profit of Company A. Good for them.

Does this mean that Company B is twice as profitable? Is it run more efficiently? Would you want to invest in it rather than Company A? Maybe you would; maybe you wouldn't. What if we extend our analysis a bit further and discover that Company A had assets of $200,000 and Company B had assets of $1,000,000? We are now in a position to see that Company A had a return on assets (ROA) of 25 percent ($50,000 ÷ $200,000 = 0.25) and Company B a return of only 10 percent ($100,000 ÷ $1,000,000 = 0.10). This changes the picture of their relative performances rather dramatically.

There is a big difference between profit and profitability. While Company B made twice the profit, it was less than half as profitable as measured by return on assets. Why? Because, as our ratio makes apparent, it used its assets less efficiently than did Company A. This simple ratio was useful in providing us with a bit more insight into these two companies.

Ratios show the relationship of one item to another. We can express this relationship between any two items that can be quantified. In order for a ratio to be relevant, however, there must be a significant relationship between the two items it compares. In a sense, then, our discussion of financial statement analysis is about relationships.

Let's suppose we have calculated the significant ratios and thoroughly analyzed the relationships between all of the relevant items on a firm's financial statements for the current year. We've made a good start. We still, however, don't know as much as we should to make informed judgments about the performance or financial health of the firm.

To get a further insight into the firm, we need to compare the results of our computations with some type of benchmark or, better yet, benchmarks. There are generally four benchmarks we might use: past performance of the company (i.e. horizontal, or trend, analysis), the performance of the best-performing companies in the same industry, industry averages, and a pre-set target. The name of the game in financial analysis is comparison, comparison, comparison.

Trend analysis compares this year's results with past years' and is useful in revealing the direction, speed and extent of trends. It allows us to compare trends in related items. For example, we can compare the rate of change in sales with the rate of change in accounts receivable. Under normal conditions we would expect them to change at roughly the same rate. If the rate of change in accounts receivable is significantly greater than the rate of change in sales we should ask why. Perhaps the firm changed its credit policy and is now extending credit to higher-risk customers. Perhaps more accounts receivable are in danger of not being collected. Similarly, the rate of change in cost of goods sold should parallel that of labor costs. If not, we should ask why.

Before going further a couple of caveats are in order: If we are comparing this year's results with those of the past several years, it is important to know if this year and/or the earlier years were normal. If the nation suffered a major terrorist attack which affected our sales or if our major factory was in the path of a tornado in one of these years, we might want to exclude that year for comparison purposes. Otherwise, our data is likely to be skewed, and comparisons will be meaningless if not misleading.

When we compare the results of one firm with those of others, the firms should all be in the same industry. In today's world of conglomerates it's not always easy to tell. Furthermore, it's not sufficient that they only be in the same industry. They must also be similar in size. The local company with 12 employees that makes computer software and Microsoft are in the same industry. They're not comparable, however. Their size differences make their financial statements too dissimilar for comparison purposes.

Also, we would want to determine if both firms use similar accounting methods. (You can determine this by reviewing the notes to their financial statements.) If both firms have large inventories and one firm uses LIFO and the other FIFO to value their inventories, they may not be comparable without first making adjustments.

If we benchmark our results against pre-set standards, we need to consider how the standards were established. Are they realistic? Are they too slack or too rigid and unobtainable?

Let's illustrate how ratio analysis can be used to gain insight into a firm by analyzing the financial statements of the Acme Corporation.

Their income statement and balance sheet are reproduced in Figures 9.1 and 9.2, respectively, for easy reference.

Financial statement ratios are often placed in four different categories: liquidity, leverage, activity and profitability.

Liquidity Ratios

Liquidity ratios are designed to measure a firm's ability to meet its current and ongoing financial obligations. A firm's degree of liquidity has important implications for its ability to carry on day-

Acme Corporation
Income Statement
For the Year Ended December 31

(000 omitted)	2009	2008
Revenues	$12,500	$11,800
Less Cost of Goods Sold	8,300	7,800
Gross Margin	4,200	4,000
Less: Selling, General and Admin. Expenses:		
Rent	630	670
Utilities	500	490
Insurance	400	380
Advertising	180	175
Depreciation	150	140
Research and Development	440	400
Operating Income	1,900	1,745
Other Income /Expense		
Interest Expense	620	650
Earnings before Tax	1,280	1,095
Income Tax	377	329
Earnings before Extraordinary Items	903	766
Extraordinary Items (net of tax)	120	—
Net Income	$783	$766
(Dividends paid, $400)		
Common Stock Price	$58	$50

Figure 9.1

Acme Corporation
Balance Sheet
As of December 31

(000 omitted)	2009	2008
Assets		
Current Assets:		
Cash	$521	$298
Accounts Receivable	1,374	1,280
Inventory	2,236	2,310
Prepaid Items	150	120
Total Current Assets	4,281	4,008
Property, Plant and Equipment		
Buildings, Machinery and Trucks	3,600	3,500
Less Accumulated Depreciation	(1,200)	(1,050)
Net Prop., Plant and Equip.	2,400	2,450
Other Assets		
Long-Term Investments	1,500	1,400
Total Assets	$8,181	$7,858
Liabilities and Stockholders' Equity		
Current Liabilities:		
Accounts Payable	$920	$950
Wages Payable	850	805
Short-Term Notes Payable	345	320
Total Current Liabilities	2,115	2,075
Long-Term Debt	1,200	1,300
Owners' Equity		
Preferred Stock ($50 par, 6%, 1,000 sh. issued)	50	50
Common Stock ($8 par, 250,000 sh. issued)	2,000	2,000
Paid-in Capital in Excess of Par	500	500
Retained Earnings	2,316	1,933
Total Liabilities and Stockholders' Equity	$8,181	$7,858

Figure 9.2

to-day business operations, pay short-term creditors, meet pay-roll, carry adequate inventory and help its customers finance their purchases.

Current ratio = current assets ÷ current liabilities. Current assets include cash and other assets which can reasonably be expected to convert to cash or be consumed during a firm's normal operating cycle. Current liabilities are debts expected to be satisfied with the use of current assets within one year or the firm's normal operating cycle. Since a firm pays its current liabilities from current assets, there is an obvious and important relationship between the two. The higher the current ratio, the more liquid the company, that is, the easier it will be for the company to meet its current financial obligations.

Being liquid sounds like a good thing and generally speaking it is. However, it's possible to be too liquid: to have too much cash, too large a balance in accounts receivable and too much inventory. Cash lying around in the bank is not earning a very good return. A large amount of accounts receivable simply means a firm is owed a lot of money, some of which it may never see, and large inventories might well mean excess inventory that isn't selling.

What is a "good" current ratio? It all depends on the nature of the company. A ratio of 2:1 means a company has twice as many current assets as current liabilities. If a firm is in a position to reliably forecast cash inflows and outflows, it may not need a current ratio that high. On the other hand, if cash inflows and outflows are irregular and hard to predict, it may need a higher current ratio.

A firm's suppliers and short-term lenders are particularly interested in a firm's liquidity. If a firm doesn't have sufficient liquidity, it may have trouble paying for inventory and find that suppliers are willing to do business only on a collect-on-delivery (C.O.D.) basis.

Acme's current ratio for 2008 is \$4,008 ÷ \$2,075 = 1.93:1. What is it for 2009?

Quick ratio = "quick assets" ÷ current liabilities. This ratio is also called the acid-test ratio because it is the acid test of a firm's liquidity. So-called quick assets include cash, accounts receivable and short-term marketable securities, in other words those assets that can most quickly be turned into cash and used to pay current liabilities. Inventories and prepaid expenses (e.g. prepaid rent and insurance) are excluded from the numerator.

The reason we exclude inventory and prepaid expenses from the numerator is that, while they are normally considered current assets, they are not necessarily liquid. To raise cash quickly by selling inventory may require a drastic reduction in prices. If you've paid rent for three months in advance and ask your landlord for a refund, you probably won't receive much more than a blank stare.

Most writers suggest that a quick ratio of 1:1 is adequate for most firms. They're probably right.

Acme's quick ratio for 2008 is $1,578 ÷ $2,075 = 0.76:1, indicating that its most liquid assets are only 76 percent of its current liabilities. What is its quick ratio for 2009?

Another measure of liquidity is not a ratio, but an absolute number.

Working capital = current assets − current liabilities. Working capital is simply the excess of current assets over current liabilities. Think of this excess as a financial safety cushion. This cushion is necessary for a firm to have enough current assets to satisfy its current obligations and to provide for possible contingencies and uncertainties.

Acme has $4,008 − $2,075 = $1,933 of working capital for 2008. How much for 2009?

Financial Leverage Ratios

Picture this: You park your car in the driveway and when you come out of the house you find that a prankster has put a 500-pound boulder behind your car. You have valuable shrubs on either side of the driveway and need to get to work. You're a big, strong guy or gal, but you're not strong enough to move a 500-pound rock. What to do? The thing to do is find a 50-pound rock and a long iron pole. Using the small rock as a fulcrum, you slip one end of the bar under the large rock and using your weight and the leverage provided by the fulcrum and the pole, you can roll the large rock away. Leverage allows you to increase the effects of your labor. Financial leverage can do the same for the owners of a company.

Consider the balance sheet equation Assets = Liabilities + Owner's Equity. Financial leverage ratios refer to the use of debt versus owners' equity in financing a firm's assets. Large debt in relation to owners' equity results in a high degree of financial leverage. The higher the degree is of financial leverage, the greater the impact a given change in revenue will have on net income, both positive and negative. Financial leverage is a two-edged sword.

If financial leverage is used properly it allows a firm's owners to earn a higher return on their investment than they otherwise would. Consider the following two examples:

> Denali Company: Net income, $10,000
> Assets $50,000 = Liabilities $30,000 + Owners' Equity $20,000.
> Blueberry Company: Net income $10,000
> Assets $50,000 = Liabilities $20,000 + Owners' Equity $30,000.

Both companies have the same amount of assets and the same net income. Furthermore, both earn a return on assets of 20 percent ($10,000 ÷ $50,000). They appear to be very much alike. Denali's owners, however, earn a return on their investment of 50 percent ($10,000 ÷ $20,000) while Blueberry's owners earn a return of only 33 percent ($10,000 ÷ $30,000). It sounds as though Denali's owners have the better deal, doesn't it? Not necessarily. Increased leverage also means increased risk. That extra debt the Denali Company has entails higher fixed costs in the form of interest. If business goes south, Denali is still going to have to make principal and interest payments on that debt.

Leverage involves a risk–reward trade-off. Increased leverage offers the opportunity for a greater return, but it's at the cost of higher risk. So what's the proper amount of risk? It's difficult, if even possible, to generalize. Part of the answer lies in the owner's attitude toward risk. Some owners are risk averse, while others are risk neutral. Gamblers tend to be risk-seekers. In general, however, investors and long-term lenders are risk averse and very interested in the amount of leverage a firm bears.

For 2008, Acme has a **debt to equity ratio** (debt ÷ equity) of ($2,075 + $1,300) ÷ ($50 + $2,000 + $500 + $1,933) = $3,375 ÷

4,483 = 0.753:1, meaning that debt is 75 percent of owners' equity. For every \$1 of financing provided by the firm's owners, creditors provided a bit over 75 cents. What is Acme's debt to equity ratio for 2009? Has it become more or less leveraged?

Another way of measuring a firm's leverage is to calculate the **debt to total assets ratio** (debt/total assets). For 2008, Acme's debt to total assets ratio was \$3,375/\$7,858 = 0.429:1. Acme financed 43 percent of its assets with debt. Creditors are very interested in a firm's leverage. The greater the degree of leverage a company has, the less protection its creditors have.

While strictly speaking not a leverage ratio, **times interest earned** is a measure that is also important to lenders. As its name implies, times interest earned indicates the number of times that net income before interest expense and income taxes exceeds interest expense. It is calculated as operating income ÷ interest expense. For 2008, Acme's times interest earned measure was \$1,745/\$650 = 2.69 times. For 2009?

Activity Ratios

Activity ratios measure the extent to which a firm uses various assets. Theoretically, there is some "right" amount of "right" assets at any given time for a firm. For example, there is some right amount of cash to have on hand. If a firm has too much cash on hand it may be forgoing profitable investment opportunities. If it has too little, it may forgo cash discounts or not have the funds to pay recurring debts or, even worse, it may not be able to meet payroll. Similar statements can also be made about inventory, accounts receivable and so on.

What the "right" amount of assets is, is hard to tell and impossible to generalize. The answer depends on such factors as the industry in which the firm competes and the firm's strategic policy. You wouldn't expect the inventory for an automobile dealer to turn over as fast as the inventory for a grocery store. Also, some firms may pursue a just-in-time inventory policy, while others prefer to stock large inventories.

Inventory turnover is calculated as cost of goods sold divided by inventory (cost of goods sold ÷ inventory). For 2008, Acme's inventory turned over $7,800 ÷ $2,310 = 3.38 times. Inventory turnover is also often calculated as cost of goods sold ÷ average inventory. We have used the ending inventory balance as of December 31 in our example. Unless inventory fluctuates a great deal during the year, either method is acceptable. What is inventory turnover for 2009? Is Acme using its inventory more or less actively?

A complementary measure is the **number of days' sales in inventory**. The number of days' sales in inventory is calculated as 365 ÷ inventory turnover (365 ÷ 3.38 = 107.9) Acme has better than three months' worth of inventory on hand. It is certainly not following a just-in-time inventory policy. How many days' sales did it have in inventory at the end of 2009?

Accounts receivable turnover is calculated as sales divided by accounts receivable (sales ÷ accounts receivable). It can also be calculated as sales ÷ average accounts receivable. For 2008, Acme's accounts receivable turnover was $11,800 ÷ 1,280 = 9.2 times. For 2009?

Is that good, bad or indifferent? We don't know, do we? To answer that question we need to know what industry we're in, what the competition is doing and what our credit policy is. At the risk of sounding like a broken record, when it comes to financial statement analysis the importance of comparison, comparison, comparison cannot be overstated.

The amount of accounts receivable a firm has depends on several factors, the most important of which are its level of sales, the credit terms it extends to customers and its efficiency in collecting accounts.

Accounts receivables illustrate perhaps better than any other asset the adage that there is some "right" amount of assets. If a company has a credit policy that is too strict, it will lose sales to competitors. If the policy is too lenient, a firm is likely to extend credit where it shouldn't and wind up with uncollectible accounts.

Acme has 39.7 days' worth of sales in accounts receivable at the end of 2008 (365 ÷ 9.2). If Acme's credit policy is 2/10, n/30, meaning it allows a 2 percent discount if the customer pays within ten days, with the balance due within 30 days from the date of sale, it has a problem. The credit manager should get to work collecting some of those old accounts or Acme will find itself with accounts that can't be collected.

In a like manner we can measure the adequacy of and the efficiency with which we manage most of our tangible assets and our liabilities by calculating turnover rates for each of them. Calculating **accounts payable turnover** (purchases divided by accounts payable) and average days' purchases in accounts payable (365 ÷ accounts payable turnover) gives us an indication if the firm is paying its obligations in a timely manner and also taking advantage of discounts. Comparing accounts payable turnover for several years will reveal if we are falling behind or keeping up with our obligations.

Let's go off on a tangent for a moment and talk about the importance of taking advantage of cash discounts. As we mentioned earlier, in an effort to encourage customers to pay in a timely fashion, businesses often provide credit terms of 2/10, n/30. How important is it to take advantage of this discount? After all it's only 2 percent. Or is it? Consider this: If you are offered these terms and pay on the 10th day you get to deduct 2 percent from the purchase price. If you do not pay by the 10th, you lose the 2 percent and now you have to pay the full amount by the 30th. That means you are paying the equivalent of 2 percent interest on your purchases for 20 additional days of credit. How many 20-day periods are there in a year? Eighteen. Two percent times 18 comes to a 36 percent effective rate of interest. That's a quite high interest rate to be paying, to say nothing of the fact that forgoing discounts does not help your overall credit rating. (If we compound that 2 percent interest every 20 days and recognize there are 365, not 360, days in a year, the interest rate is actually closer to 36.5 percent.)

Profitability Ratios

Profitability ratios relate some measure of a firm's profit to some factor involved in the earning process. Let's look at five different profitability ratios.

Return on assets (ROA) compares net income to total assets.

ROA is calculated as net income divided by total assets (net income ÷ total assets). Before we go further, we should reiterate that different authors and analysts use different measures of net income and total assets. Some authors use net income minus interest (net of taxes) in the numerator; some merely use operating income. Many use average assets in the denominator. Regardless of how the numerator and denominator are defined, ROA, in one way or another, relates the income earned during a period of time to the assets that were invested to generate those earnings. Whichever formula you use, the important point is to be consistent in your analysis.

During the 1930s, analysts at E.I. DuPont de Nemours & Co. developed what has become known as the DuPont method of calculating ROA. The DuPont method recognizes that, in order to earn a satisfactory ROA, management must do two things simultaneously: earn a satisfactory profit margin and efficiently utilize the assets at their disposal. The calculations involved in the DuPont method are:

ROA = Asset Turnover × Profit Margin, that is
ROA = (Sales ÷ Total Assets) × (Net Income ÷ Sales)

When one looks through the lens of the DuPont method and considers there are really two components to ROA, it becomes clear that a firm with a high asset turnover and low profit margin (say, a fish market) can enjoy the same ROA as a firm with a low asset turnover and high profit margin (say, a jeweler).

In 2008, Acme had an asset turnover (sales divided by total assets) of $11,800 ÷ $7,858 = 1.50 and a profit margin (net income divided by sales) of $766 ÷ $11,800 = 0.065. Acme's ROA was 1.50 × 0.065 = 0.0975 or 9.75 percent. Use the DuPont method and calculate Acme's ROA for 2009.

Return on common stockholders' equity (ROE) compares net income minus preferred dividends to common stockholders' equity [(net income − preferred stock dividends) ÷ common stockholders' equity]. ROE is important to both current and prospective stockholders because it relates income to the owners' investment.

If a firm has no debt and no preferred stock, its return on assets and its return on equity will be the same. That is, 100 percent of the firm's assets will be funded by the owners. Hence, the firm's owners will not have the benefits or risks inherent with financial leverage.

This, of course, is rarely the case. Most companies have debt. The use of debt creates financial leverage. Recall from our earlier discussion of leverage ratios that the judicious use of debt allows the owners of a firm to enjoy a return on their equity that is greater than the firm's return on assets. Also keep in mind the risk–reward trade-off. The more debt a firm has, the greater its leverage and the greater its risk.

Acme's income in 2008 was $766,000; it paid preferred dividends of $3,000 ($50,000 × 0.06). The income accruing to common stockholders was therefore $763,000. The firm's ROE was 17.21 percent [$763,000 ÷ ($2,000,000 + $500,000 + $1,933,000)]. The difference between the ROA of 9.75 percent and the ROE of 17.21 percent was due to leverage. Recall that Acme had a debt to asset ratio of 0.429:1 in 2008. It appears that Acme has used debt wisely and to the benefit of the stockholders. How does Acme's ROE for 2009 compare?

A firm's **profit margin** relates net income to sales (net income ÷ sales). It shows the percentage of each sales dollar that results in net income. Remember that profit margin is part of the DuPont method of calculating return on assets. Companies such as grocery stores like to point out to consumers that they have low profit margins. We needn't feel too sorry for them. They also have relatively high inventory and total asset turnover, thereby earning satisfactory returns on assets.

Don't confuse profit margin with gross margin. Gross margin is not a ratio at all. Nor is it a percentage of anything. It is merely the difference between sales and cost of goods sold. Acme's profit margin for 2008 was 6.5 percent ($766 ÷ $11,800). For 2009?

A firm's **earnings per share** (EPS) (net income − preferred dividends ÷ average number of common shares outstanding) is of particular interest to stockholders and potential investors because of its importance in determining the market value of a share of common stock. The calculation of EPS can be straightforward or quite complicated depending on the firm's capital structure. The term "capital structure" refers to how the firm finances its assets. In addition to raising funds through the sale of common stock, a firm with a complex capital structure might have also used several different issues of preferred stock, stock warrants and long-term bonds.

Entire chapters of intermediate accounting texts are sometimes given to the calculation of fully diluted EPS. Depending on their capital structure, firms may be required to publish two different EPS figures, basic and fully diluted. Many large corporations have quite complicated capital structures with financial instruments such as bonds, warrants and preferred stocks that may or may not be convertible into common stock under varying conditions. In such cases, the firm will have to calculate EPS as though these conversions had been made. These calculations result in a diluted earnings per share figure. Acme has a simple capital structure and would not be required to calculate diluted EPS.

Basic EPS is calculated as net income less preferred dividends, divided by the weighted average number of shares of common stock outstanding. Acme's preferred dividends were $3,000 for both 2008 and 2009 ($50 × 1,000 × 0.06) Since Acme neither bought nor sold shares of its stock in 2008, its EPS was ($766,000 − $3,000) ÷ 250,000 = $3.05. How did it do in 2009?

A firm's **price/earnings ratio** (P/E ratio) compares the price of the firm's common stock on any given day with its earnings per share for the most recent year (current market price ÷ EPS). The P/E ratio is sometimes referred to as the firm's **earnings multiple**. To understand the significance of the P/E ratio, we must consider how stock prices are determined. The primary determinant of the price of a company's stock is investors' expectations about the future earnings of the company. If investors in general believe the company's future earnings will be good, they will bid the price of the stock up. If they do not believe the company's earnings will be good, they will sell the stock, and its price and P/E ratio will decline. If a firm has an above-average P/E ratio it is probably because investors anticipate increased earnings.

Look at the stock listings in the *Wall Street Journal* or the business section of any major newspaper. There will be a column showing the P/E ratio for all listed companies. Note the wide range of ratios. It is not unusual to see investors paying more than 30 times earnings for the stock of some companies and less than 10 times for other companies. Clearly, investors as a whole are far more optimistic about the future of some firms than they are of others. Sometimes they are too optimistic. It does not follow that you should buy stock in a firm with a high P/E ratio. Indeed, quite the opposite is often true. In 2008, Acme had a P/E ratio of 16.39:1 ($50 ÷ $3.05).

A copy of selected portions of Columbia Sportswear Company's 10-K report for 2009 is shown in Appendix A. The annual report on Form 10-K includes audited financial statements and footnotes. Together they provide a comprehensive overview of the company's business and financial condition. Federal securities laws require publicly traded companies such as Columbia Sportswear to disclose this information on an ongoing basis.

Summary

Managers as well as investors and creditors can improve their understanding and the performance of a firm's operations and prospects by developing their ability to analyze and understand financial statements. This chapter presents financial ratios as a means of analyzing and gaining insight into the operations of a firm.

Ratios show the relationship of one item to another. In order for a ratio to be relevant there needs to be a significant relationship between the two items it compares. This chapter breaks ratios down into four types: liquidity, which measures a firm's ability to meet current ongoing financial obligations; activity, which measures how actively a firm uses its various resources; leverage, which compares its debt and equity financing; and profitability, which relates a firm's profit to some factor involved in the earning process.

Financial ratio analysis relies heavily on comparison of data. The more relevant comparisons an analyst or manager can make, the more insight and understanding he or she will have. For a thorough analysis, an individual firm's ratios need to be compared with other ratios. For example, a firm's current year's ratios can be compared with its ratios from prior years to determine trends, ratios of similar firms in the same industry, and budgeted ratios, which provide benchmarks for measuring relative performance.

Exercises

1 What do liquidity ratios reveal?

2 What is Columbia Sportswear's (C.S.) current ratio for 2009? Has it become more liquid?

3 What is C.S.'s quick ratio for 2009? Does this confirm your finding in exercise 2?

4 What do leverage ratios reveal?

5 What is C.S.'s debt to equity ratio in 2009?

6 What is the ratio of C.S.'s assets to debt in 2009?

7 What was C.S.'s times interest earned ratio for 2008 and for 2009?

8 Is C.S. more or less leveraged in 2009 as compared with 2008? As a banker, would you be more or less likely to make a loan to them in 2009 as opposed to 2008?

9 What do activity ratios reveal?

10 What are C.S.'s inventory turnover and their number of days' sales in inventory for 2009?

11 Compare C.S.'s accounts receivable turnover for 2008 with their result for 2009.

12 Did they turn their accounts more quickly in 2009?

13 Compare C.S.'s accounts payable turnover for 2008 with their result for 2009. What do your results imply?

14 What do profitability ratios reveal?

15 Using the DuPont method, calculate C.S.'s return on assets for 2009. How did they do compared with 2008?

16 What is C.S.'s return on equity for 2009? Compare your results with your results in exercise 15. What are the implications of this comparison?

APPENDIX A

PORTIONS OF COLUMBIA SPORTSWEAR'S 2009 10-K REPORT

UNITED STATES SECURITIES AND EXCHANGE COMMISSION

Washington, DC 20549

FORM 10-K

☒ ANNUAL REPORT PURSUANT TO SECTION 13 OR 15(D) OF THE SECURITIES EXCHANGE ACT OF 1934

For the fiscal year ended December 31, 2009

COLUMBIA SPORTSWEAR COMPANY

(Exact name of registrant as specified in its charter)

Oregon	93–0498284
(State or other jurisdiction of incorporation or organization)	(IRS Employer Identification Number)
14375 NW Science Park Drive Portland, Oregon	97229
(Address of principal executive offices)	(Zip Code)

(503) 985–4000

(Registrant's telephone number, including area code)

Securities registered pursuant to Section 12(b) of the Act:

Title of each class	Name of each exchange on which registered
Common Stock	The NASDAQ Stock Market LLC

Securities registered pursuant to Section 12(g) of the Act: None

Indicate by check mark if the registrant is a well-known seasoned issuer, as defined in Rule 405 of the Securities Act.   Yes ☐   No ☒

Indicate by check mark if the registrant is not required to file reports pursuant to Section 13 or Section 15(d) of the Act. Yes ☐   No ☒

Indicate by check mark whether the registrant (1) has filed all reports required to be filed by Section 13 or 15(d) of the Securities Exchange Act of 1934 during the preceding 12 months (or for such shorter period that the registrant was required to file such reports), and (2) has been subject to such filing requirements for the past 90 days.   Yes ☒   No ☐

Indicate by check mark whether the registrant has submitted electronically and posted on its corporate web site, if any, every Interactive Data File required to be submitted and posted pursuant to Rule 405 of Regulation S-T during the preceding 12 months (or for such short period that the registrant was required to submit and post such files).   Yes ☐   No ☐

Indicate by check mark if disclosure of delinquent filers pursuant to Item 405 of Regulation S-K is not contained herein, and will not be contained, to the best of registrant's knowledge, in definitive proxy or information statements incorporated by reference in Part III of this Form 10-K or any amendment to this Form 10-K.   ☒

Indicate by check mark whether the registrant is a large accelerated filer, an accelerated filer, a non-accelerated filer, or a smaller reporting company. See the definitions of "large accelerated filer," "accelerated filer" and "smaller reporting company" in Rule 12b-2 of the Exchange Act.

Large accelerated filer ☐   Accelerated filer ☒
Non-accelerated filer ☐ (Do not check if a   Smaller reporting
        smaller reporting company)   company ☐

Indicate by check mark whether the registrant is a shell company (as defined in Rule 12b-2 of the Exchange Act).   Yes ☐   No ☒

The aggregate market value of the voting common stock held by non-affiliates of the registrant as of June 30, 2009, the last business day of the registrant's most recently completed second fiscal quarter, was $357,113,000 based on the last reported sale price of the Company's Common Stock as reported by the NASDAQ Global Select Market System on that day.

The number of shares of Common Stock outstanding on February 26, 2010 was 33,706,791.

Part III is incorporated by reference from the registrant's proxy statement for its 2010 annual meeting of shareholders to be filed with the Commission within 120 days of December 31, 2009.

COLUMBIA SPORTSWEAR COMPANY

CONSOLIDATED BALANCE SHEETS
(In thousands)

	December 31,	
	2009	2008
ASSETS		
Current Assets:		
Cash and cash equivalents	$ 86,664	$ 230,617
Short-term investments	22,759	22,433
Accounts receivable, net (Note 2)	226,548	299,585
Inventories, net (Note 3)	222,161	256,312
Deferred income taxes (Note 9)	31,550	33,867
Prepaid expenses and other current assets	32,030	29,705
Total current assets	921,712	872,519
Property, plant, and equipment, net (Note 4)	235,440	229,693
Intangibles and other non-current assets (Notes 2 and 9)	43,072	33,365
Goodwill (Note 2)	12,659	12,659
Total assets	$ 1,212,883	$ 1,148,236
LIABILITIES AND SHAREHOLDERS' EQUITY		
Current Liabilities:		
Accounts payable	$ 102,494	$ 104,354
Accrued liabilities (Note 6)	67,312	58,148
Income taxes payable (Note 9)	6,884	8,718
Deferred income taxes (Note 9)	2,597	1,969
Total current liabilities	179,287	173,189
Income taxes payable (Note 9)	19,830	20,412
Deferred income taxes (Note 9)	1,494	—
Other long-term liabilities (Note 7)	15,044	10,545
Total liabilities	215,655	204,146
Commitments and contingencies (Note 11)		

Shareholders' Equity:

Preferred stock; 10,000 shares authorized; none issued and outstanding	—	—
Common stock (no par value); 125,000 shares authorized; 33,736 and 33,865 issued and outstanding (Note 8)	836	1,481
Retained earnings (Note 8)	952,948	909,443
Accumulated other comprehensive income (Note 14)	43,444	33,166
Total shareholders' equity	997,228	944,090
Total liabilities and shareholders' equity	$ 1,212,883	$ 1,148,236

See accompanying notes to consolidated financial statements.

COLUMBIA SPORTSWEAR COMPANY

CONSOLIDATED STATEMENTS OF OPERATIONS
(In thousands, except per share amounts)

	Year Ended December 31,		
	2009	2008	2007
Net sales	$1,244,023	$1,317,835	$1,356,039
Cost of sales	719,945	750,024	776,288
Gross profit	524,078	567,811	579,751
Selling, general, and administrative expenses	444,715	430,350	385,769
Impairment of acquired intangible assets (Note 2)	—	24,742	—
Net licensing income	8,399	5,987	5,157
Income from operations	87,762	118,706	199,139
Interest income, net	2,088	7,537	8,888
Income before income tax	89,850	126,243	208,027
Income tax expense (Note 9)	(22,829)	(31,196)	(63,575)
Net income	$ 67,021	$ 95,047	$ 144,452
Earnings per share:			
Basic	$ 1.98	$ 2.75	$ 4.00
Diluted	1.97	2.74	3.96
Cash dividends per share:	$ 0.66	$ 0.64	$ 0.58
Weighted average shares outstanding (Note 13):			
Basic	33,846	34,610	36,106
Diluted	33,981	34,711	36,434

See accompanying notes to consolidated financial statements.

COLUMBIA SPORTSWEAR COMPANY

CONSOLIDATED STATEMENTS OF CASH FLOWS
(In thousands)

	Year Ended December 31,		
	2009	2008	2007
Cash flows from operating activities:			
Net income	$ 67,021	$ 95,047	$ 144,452
Adjustments to reconcile net income to net cash provided by operating activities:			
Depreciation and amortization	36,253	31,158	30,338
Loss on disposal or impairment of property, plant, and equipment	1,828	253	237
Deferred income tax (benefit) expense	55	(10,338)	278
Stock-based compensation	6,353	6,302	7,260
Excess tax benefit from employee stock plans	(41)	(72)	(1,811)
Impairment of acquired intangibles	—	24,742	—
Changes in operating assets and liabilities:			
Accounts receivable	77,490	(9,689)	(3,093)
Inventories	38,831	4,507	(46,010)
Prepaid expenses and other current assets	(1,695)	(15,787)	(1,355)
Intangibles and other assets	(5,179)	101	592
Accounts payable	(16,944)	8,944	1,381
Accrued liabilities	7,563	(1,047)	(4,400)
Income taxes payable	(1,558)	2,567	(5,665)
Other liabilities	4,395	8,242	2,111
Net cash provided by operating activities	214,372	144,930	124,315
Cash flows from investing activities:			
Purchases of short-term investments	(25,305)	(72,337)	(305,769)
Sales of short-term investments	25,163	131,565	379,460

Capital expenditures	(33,074)	(47,580)	(31,971)
Proceeds from sale of property, plant, and equipment	31	52	32
Net cash provided by (used in) investing activities	(33,185)	11,700	41,752
Cash flows from financing activities:			
Proceeds from notes payable	57,588	33,727	30,651
Repayments on notes payable	(57,588)	(33,727)	(34,276)
Repayment on long-term debt and other long-term liabilities	(4)	(21)	(22)
Proceeds from issuance of common stock under employee stock plans, net	86	3,488	14,162
Excess tax benefit from employee stock plans	41	72	1,811
Repurchase of common stock	(7,399)	(83,865)	(31,819)
Cash dividends paid	(22,331)	(22,098)	(20,915)
Net cash used in financing activities	(29,607)	(102,424)	(40,408)
Net effect of exchange rate changes on cash	4,467	(15,539)	1,411
Net increase in cash and cash equivalents	156,047	38,667	127,070
Cash and cash equivalents, beginning of year	230,617	191,950	64,880
Cash and cash equivalents, end of year	$ 386,664	$ 230,617	$ 191,950
Supplemental disclosures of cash flow information:			
Cash paid during the year for interest, net of capitalized interest	$ 35	$ 47	$ 148
Cash paid during the year for income taxes	31,284	48,521	73,293
Supplemental disclosures of non-cash investing activities:			
Capital expenditures incurred but not yet paid	7,852	6,760	2,318

See accompanying notes to consolidated financial statements.

APPENDIX A

COLUMBIA SPORTSWEAR COMPANY

NOTES TO CONSOLIDATED FINANCIAL STATEMENTS

Note 1 – Basis of Presentation and Organization

Nature of the business:

Columbia Sportswear Company is a global leader in the design, development, marketing and distribution of active outdoor apparel, including sportswear, outerwear, footwear, accessories and equipment.

Principles of consolidation:

The consolidated financial statements include the accounts of Columbia Sportswear Company and its wholly-owned subsidiaries (the "Company"). All significant intercompany balances and transactions have been eliminated in consolidation.

Estimates and assumptions:

The preparation of financial statements in conformity with accounting principles generally accepted in the United States of America requires management to make estimates and assumptions that affect the reported amounts of assets and liabilities and disclosure of contingent assets and liabilities at the date of the consolidated financial statements and the reported amounts of revenues and expenses during the reporting period. Actual results may differ from these estimates and assumptions. Some of these more significant estimates relate to revenue recognition, allowance for doubtful accounts, inventory, product warranty, long-lived and intangible assets and income taxes.

Reclassifications:

Certain immaterial reclassifications of amounts reported in the prior period financial statements have been made to conform to classifications used in the current period financial statements.

Dependence on key suppliers:

The Company's products are produced by independent factories worldwide. For 2009, the Company sourced nearly all of its products outside the United States, principally in the Southeast Asia. In 2009, the Company's four largest apparel factory groups accounted for approximately 15% of the Company's total global apparel production and the Company's four largest footwear factory groups accounted for approximately 66% of the Company's total global footwear production. In addition, a single vendor supplied substantially all of the zippers used in the Company's products in 2009. From time to time, the Company has had difficulty satisfying its raw material and finished goods requirements. Although the Company believes that it can identify and qualify additional raw material suppliers and independent factories to produce these products, the unavailability of some existing suppliers or independent factories for supply of these products may have a material adverse effect on the Company.

Concentration of credit risk:

Trade Receivables

At December 31, 2009, the Company had one customer in its Canadian segment that accounted for approximately 15.5% of consolidated accounts receivable. At December 31, 2008, the Company had one customer in its EMEA segment and one customer in its Canadian segment that accounted for approximately 13.5% and 10.2% of consolidated accounts receivable, respectively. No single customer accounted for 10% or more of consolidated revenues for any of the years ended December 31, 2009, 2008 or 2007.

Cash and Investments

At December 31, 2009, approximately 80% of the Company's cash and cash equivalents were concentrated in domestic and international money market mutual funds. Substantially all of the Company's money market mutual funds were assigned a AAA or analogous rating from S&P, Moody's Investor Services ("Moody's") or Fitch Ratings.

All the Company's remaining cash and cash equivalents and short-term investments were deposited with various institutions in the Company's primary operating geographies. All institutions were rated investment grade by both S&P and Moody's and most were rated AA- / Aa1 or better.

Derivatives

The Company uses derivative instruments primarily to hedge the exchange rate risk of anticipated transactions denominated in non-functional currencies. From time to time, the Company also uses derivative instruments to economically hedge the exchange rate risk of certain investment positions and to hedge balance sheet remeasurement risk. At December 31, 2009, the Company's derivative contracts had a remaining maturity of approximately one year or less. All the counterparties to these transactions had a S&P / Moody's short-term credit rating of A-2 / P-2 or better. The net exposure to any single counterparty, which is generally limited to the aggregate unrealized gain of all contracts with that counterparty, was less than $1,000,000 at December 31, 2009. The majority of the Company's derivative counterparties have strong credit ratings and as a result, the Company does not require collateral to facilitate transactions. See Note 16 for further disclosures concerning derivatives.

Note 2 – Summary of Significant Accounting Policies

Cash and cash equivalents:

Cash and cash equivalents are stated at cost, which approximates fair value, and include investments with maturities of three months or less from the date of acquisition. At December 31, 2009 and 2008, cash and cash equivalents were $386,664,000 and $230,617,000, respectively, primarily consisting of money market funds and time deposits with maturities ranging from overnight to less than 90 days.

Investments:

At December 31, 2009 and 2008, short-term investments consisted of shares in a short-term bond fund available for use in current operations and time deposits with maturities of six months or less. All short-term investments are classified as available-for-sale securities and are recorded at fair value with any unrealized gains and losses reported, net of tax, in other comprehensive income. Realized gains or losses are determined based on the specific identification method.

At December 31, 2009, long-term investments consisted of mutual fund shares held to offset liabilities to participants in the Company's deferred compensation plan. The investments are classified as long-term as the related deferred compensation liabilities are not expected to be paid within the next year. These investments are classified as trading securities and are recorded at fair value with unrealized gains and losses reported in operating expenses. These long-term investments are included in intangibles and other non-current assets and totaled $826,000 at December 31, 2009, including unrealized gains of $130,000. There were no long-term investments at December 31, 2008.

Accounts receivable:

Accounts receivable have been reduced by an allowance for doubtful accounts. The Company makes ongoing estimates of the uncollectibility of accounts receivable and maintains an allowance for estimated losses resulting from the inability of the Company's customers to make required payments. The allowance for doubtful accounts was $7,347,000 and $9,542,000 at December 31, 2009 and 2008, respectively.

Inventories:

Inventories are carried at the lower of cost or market. Cost is determined using the first-in, first-out method. The Company periodically reviews its inventories for excess, close-out or slow moving items and makes provisions as necessary to properly reflect inventory value.

Property, plant, and equipment:

Property, plant and equipment are stated at cost, net of accumulated depreciation. Depreciation is provided using the straight-line method over the estimated useful lives of the assets. The principal estimated useful lives are: buildings and building improvements, 15–30 years; land improvements, 15 years; furniture and fixtures, 3–10 years; and machinery and equipment, 3–5 years. Leasehold improvements are depreciated over the lesser of the estimated useful life of the improvement, which is most commonly 7 years, or the remaining term of the underlying lease.

The interest-carrying costs of capital assets under construction are capitalized based on the Company's weighted average borrowing rates if there are any outstanding borrowings. There was no capitalized interest for the years ended December 31, 2009, 2008 and 2007.

Impairment of long-lived assets:

Long-lived assets are amortized over their useful lives and are measured for impairment only when events or circumstances indicate the carrying value may be impaired. In these cases, the Company estimates the future undiscounted cash flows to be derived from the asset or asset group to determine whether a potential impairment exists. When reviewing for retail store impairment, identifiable cash flows are measured at the individual store level. If the sum of the estimated undiscounted cash flows is less than the carrying value of the asset, the Company recognizes an impairment loss, measured as the amount by which the carrying value exceeds the estimated fair value of the asset. Impairment charges for long-lived assets are included in selling, general and administrative expense and were immaterial for the years ended December 31, 2009, 2008 and 2007.

Intangibles and other non-current assets:

Intangible assets with indefinite useful lives are not amortized and are periodically evaluated for impairment. Intangible assets that are determined to have finite lives are amortized using the straight-line method over their useful lives.

The following table summarizes the Company's identifiable intangible assets (in thousands):

	December 31, 2009		December 31, 2008	
	Gross Carrying Amount	Accumulated Amortization	Gross Carrying Amount	Accumulated Amortization
Intangible assets subject to amortization:				
Patents	$ 898	$ (643)	$ 898	$ (534)
Intangible assets not subject to amortization:				
Trademarks and trade names	$ 26,872		$ 26,872	
Goodwill	12,659		12,659	
	$ 39,531		$ 39,531	

Amortization expense for the years ended December 31, 2009, 2008, and 2007 was $109,000, $205,000 and $175,000, respectively. Amortization expense for patents is estimated to be $109,000 in 2010 and $73,000 per year in 2011 and 2012. These patents are anticipated to become fully amortized in 2012.

Other non-current assets consisted of the following (in thousands):

	December 31,	
	2009	2008
Deferred tax assets	$ 5,435	$ 723
Long-term deposits	8,360	4,483
Other	2,150	923
	$ 15,945	$ 6,129

Impairment of goodwill and intangible assets:

Goodwill and intangible assets with indefinite useful lives are not amortized but instead are measured for impairment. The Company reviews and tests its goodwill and intangible assets with indefinite useful lives for impairment in the fourth quarter of each year and when events or changes in circumstances indicate that the carrying amount of such assets may be impaired. The Company's intangible assets with indefinite lives consist of trademarks and trade names. Substantially all of the Company's goodwill is recorded in the United States segment and impairment testing for goodwill is performed at the reporting unit level. The two-step process first compares the estimated fair value of reporting unit goodwill with the carrying amount of that reporting unit. The Company estimates the fair value of its reporting units using a combination of discounted cash flow analysis, comparisons with the market values of similar publicly traded companies and other operating performance based valuation methods. If step one indicates impairment, step two compares the estimated fair value of the reporting unit to the estimated fair value of all reporting unit assets and liabilities except goodwill to determine the implied fair value of goodwill. The Company calculates impairment as the excess of carrying amount of goodwill over the implied fair value of goodwill. In the impairment test for trademarks, the Company compares the estimated fair value of the asset to the carrying amount. The fair value of trademarks is estimated using the relief from royalty approach, a standard form of discounted cash flow analysis used in the valuation of trademarks. If the carrying amount of trademarks exceeds the estimated fair value, the Company calculates impairment as the excess of carrying amount over the estimate of fair value. Impairment charges are classified as a component of operating expense. The fair value estimates are based on a number of factors, including assumptions and estimates for projected sales, income, cash flows, discount rates and other operating performance measures. Changes in estimates or the application of alternative assumptions could produce significantly different results. These assumptions and estimates may change in the future due to changes in economic conditions, changes in the Company's ability to meet sales and profitability objectives or changes in the Company's business operations or strategic direction.

Intangible assets that are determined to have finite lives are amortized over their useful lives and are measured for impairment only when events or circumstances indicate the carrying value may be impaired. In these cases, the Company estimates the future undiscounted cash flows to be derived from the asset or asset group to determine whether a potential impairment exists. If the sum of the estimated undiscounted cash flows is less than the carrying value of the asset the Company recognizes an impairment loss, measured as the amount by which the carrying value exceeds the estimated fair value of the asset. Impairment charges are classified as a component of operating expense.

At December 31, 2009, the Company determined that its goodwill and intangible assets were not impaired. At December 31, 2008, the Company determined that its Pacific Trail brand and Montrail brand goodwill and trademarks were impaired. These brands were not achieving their sales and profitability objectives. The deterioration in the macroeconomic environment and the resulting effect on consumer demand decreased the probability of realizing the objectives in the near future. These brands were acquired in 2006. For the year ended December 31, 2008, the Company recorded impairment charges, before income taxes, of $12,250,000 in trademarks and $3,900,000 in goodwill for the Pacific Trail brand. The Pacific Trail brand has $2,300,000 in trademarks and no goodwill after the impairment charge. The Pacific Trail brand is a reporting unit for goodwill impairment testing and Pacific Trail brand intangible assets are included in the United States segment. For the year ended December 31, 2008, the Company recorded impairment charges, before income taxes, of $7,400,000 in trademarks, $714,000 in goodwill and $478,000 in patents for the Montrail brand. The Montrail brand has $2,600,000 in trademarks and no goodwill or patents after the impairment charge. The Montrail brand is a reporting unit for goodwill impairment testing and Montrail brand intangible assets are included in the United States segment. Other than Pacific Trail brand goodwill and trademarks and Montrail brand goodwill, trademarks and patents, at December 31, 2008, the Company determined that its goodwill and intangible assets were not impaired.

Deferred income taxes:

Income tax expense is provided at the U.S. tax rate on financial statement earnings, adjusted for the difference between the U.S. tax rate and the rate of tax in effect for non-U.S. earnings deemed to be permanently reinvested in the Company's non-U.S. operations. Deferred income taxes have not been provided for the potential remittance of non-U.S. undistributed earnings to the extent those earnings are deemed to be permanently reinvested, or to the extent such recognition would result in a deferred tax asset. Deferred income taxes are provided for the expected tax consequences of temporary differences between the tax bases of assets and liabilities and their reported amounts. Valuation allowances are recorded to reduce deferred tax assets to the amount that will more likely than not be realized.

Revenue Recognition:

The Company records wholesale and licensed product revenues when title passes and the risks and rewards of ownership have passed to the customer, based on the terms of sale. Title generally passes upon shipment to, or upon receipt by, the customer depending on the country of the sale and the agreement with the customer. Retail store revenues are recorded at the time of sale and e-commerce revenues are recorded upon shipment to the customer.

In some countries outside of the United States where title passes upon receipt by the customer, predominantly in the Company's Western European wholesale business, precise information regarding the date of receipt by the customer is not readily available. In these cases, the Company estimates the date of receipt by the customer based on historical and expected delivery times by geographic location. The Company periodically tests the accuracy of these estimates based on actual transactions. Delivery times vary by geographic location, generally from one to five days. To date, the Company has found these estimates to be materially accurate.

At the time of revenue recognition, the Company also provides for estimated sales returns and miscellaneous claims from customers as reductions to revenues. The estimates are based on historical rates of product returns and claims. However, actual returns and claims in any future period are inherently uncertain and thus may differ from the estimates. If actual or expected future returns and claims are significantly greater or lower than the reserves that had been established, the Company would record a reduction or increase to net revenues in the period in which it made such determination. Over the three year period ended December 31, 2009, the Company's actual annual sales returns and miscellaneous claims from customers have averaged approximately two percent of net sales. The allowance for outstanding sales returns and miscellaneous claims from customers was approximately $13,889,000 and $10,583,000 as of December 31, 2009 and 2008, respectively.

Cost of sales:

The expenses that are included in cost of sales include all direct product and conversion-related costs, and costs related to shipping, duties and importation. Product warranty costs and specific provisions for excess, close-out or slow moving inventory are also included in cost of sales.

Selling, general and administrative expense:

Selling, general and administrative expense consists of commissions, advertising, other selling costs, personnel-related costs, planning, receiving finished goods, warehousing, depreciation and other general operating expenses.

Shipping and handling costs:

Shipping and handling fees billed to customers are recorded as revenue. The direct costs associated with shipping goods to customers are recorded as cost of sales. Inventory planning, receiving and handling costs are recorded as a component of selling, general, and administrative expenses and were $55,867,000, $57,700,000 and $64,420,000 for the years ended December 31, 2009, 2008 and 2007, respectively.

Foreign currency translation:

The assets and liabilities of the Company's foreign subsidiaries have been translated into U.S. dollars using the exchange rates in effect at period end, and the net sales and expenses have been translated into U.S. dollars using average exchange rates in effect during the period. The foreign currency translation adjustments are included as a separate component of accumulated other comprehensive income (loss) in shareholders' equity and are not currently adjusted for income taxes when they relate to indefinite net investments in non-U.S. operations.

Fair value of financial instruments:

The carrying value of substantially all financial instruments potentially subject to valuation risk (principally consisting of cash and cash equivalents, short-term investments, accounts receivable and accounts payable) approximates fair value because of their short-term maturities. See note 17 for more information on fair value measures for financial instruments.

Derivatives:

Changes in fair values of outstanding cash flow hedges are recorded in other comprehensive income until earnings are affected by the hedged transaction. In most cases amounts recorded in other comprehensive income will be released to earnings some time after maturity of the related derivative. The Consolidated Statement of Operations classification of effective hedge results is the same as that of the underlying exposure. Results of hedges of product costs are recorded in cost of sales when the underlying hedged transaction affects earnings. Unrealized derivative gains and losses, which are recorded in current assets and liabilities, respectively, are non-cash items and therefore are taken into account in the preparation of the Consolidated Statement of Cash Flows based on their respective balance sheet classifications. See note 16 for more information on derivatives and risk management.

Stock-based compensation:

Stock-based compensation cost is estimated at the grant date based on the award's fair value and is recognized as expense over the requisite service period using the straight-line attribution method. The Company estimates stock-based compensation for stock options granted using the Black-Scholes option pricing model, which requires various highly subjective assumptions, including volatility and expected option life. Further, the Company estimates forfeitures for stock-based awards granted, which are not expected to vest. If any of these inputs or assumptions changes significantly, stock-based compensation expense may differ materially in the future from that recorded in the current period.

Advertising costs:

Advertising costs are expensed in the period incurred and are included in selling, general and administrative expenses. Total advertising expense, including cooperative advertising costs, was $65,204,000, $72,237,000 and $55,290,000 for the years ended December 31, 2009, 2008 and 2007, respectively.

Through cooperative advertising programs, the Company reimburses its wholesale customers for some of their costs of advertising the Company's products based on various criteria, including the value of purchases from the Company and various advertising specifications. Cooperative advertising costs are included in expenses because the Company receives an identifiable benefit in exchange for the cost, the advertising may be obtained from a party other than the customer, and the fair value of the advertising benefit can be reasonably estimated. Cooperative advertising costs were $10,978,000, $16,351,000 and $17,884,000 for the years ended December 31, 2009, 2008 and 2007, respectively.

Product warranty:

Some of the Company's products carry limited warranty provisions for defects in quality and workmanship. A warranty reserve is established at the time of sale to cover estimated costs based on the Company's history of warranty repairs and replacements and is recorded in cost of sales. The reserve for warranty claims at December 31, 2009 and 2008 was $12,112,000 and $9,746,000, respectively.

Recent Accounting Pronouncements:

In June 2009, the Financial Accounting Standards Board ("FASB") issued SFAS No. 168, *The FASB Accounting Standards Codification™ and the Hierarchy of Generally Accepted Accounting Principles, as amended,* which was codified into Topic 105 *Generally Accepted Accounting Standards* in the ASC. This standard establishes the FASB ASC as the source of authoritative accounting principles recognized by the FASB to be applied in the preparation of financial statements in conformity with generally accepted accounting principles. This standard is effective for interim and annual financial periods ending after September 15, 2009. The adoption of this standard did not have a material effect on the Company's consolidated financial position, results of operations or cash flows.

In May 2009, the FASB issued SFAS No. 165, *Subsequent Events,* which was codified into Topic 855 *Subsequent Events* in the ASC and updated by Accounting Standards Update No. 2010–09, *Amendments to Certain Recognition and Disclosure Requirements.* This guidance establishes general standards of evaluating and accounting for events that occur after the balance sheet date but before financial statements are issued or are available to be issued. This standard is effective for interim or annual financial periods ending after June 15, 2009. The adoption of this standard did not have a material effect on the Company's consolidated financial position, results of operations or cash flows.

In March 2008, the FASB issued SFAS No. 161, *Disclosures about Derivative Instruments and Hedging Activities,* which was codified into Topic 815 *Derivatives and Hedging* in the ASC. This standard is intended to improve financial reporting about derivative instruments and hedging activities by requiring enhanced disclosures to enable investors to better understand their effects on an entity's financial position, financial performance and cash flows. The provisions of this standard are effective for fiscal years and interim quarters beginning after November 15, 2008. The adoption of this standard did not have a material effect on the Company's consolidated financial position, results of operations or cash flows. See Note 16.

Note 3 – Inventories, Net

Inventories consist of the following (in thousands):

	December 31, 2009	December 31, 2008
Raw materials	$ 1,021	$ 621
Work in process	163	1,065
Finished goods	220,977	254,626
	$ 222,161	$ 256,312

Note 4 – Property, Plant, and Equipment, Net

Property, plant, and equipment consist of the following (in thousands):

	December 31, 2009	December 31, 2008
Land and improvements	$ 16,557	$ 16,465
Building and improvements	147,093	143,997
Machinery and equipment	184,721	171,091
Furniture and fixtures	44,158	37,886
Leasehold improvements	57,866	45,231
Construction in progress	8,932	5,929
	459,327	420,599
Less accumulated depreciation	223,887	190,906
	$ 235,440	$ 229,693

Note 5 – Short-term Borrowings and Credit Lines

The Company has available an unsecured and committed revolving line of credit providing for borrowings in an aggregate amount not to exceed, at any time, $100,000,000 during the period of August 15 through November 14 and $25,000,000 at all other times. The maturity date of this agreement is July 1, 2010. Interest, payable monthly, is computed at the bank's prime rate minus 195 to 205 basis points per annum or LIBOR plus 45 to 65 basis points. The unsecured revolving line of credit requires the Company to comply with certain covenants including a Capital Ratio, which limits indebtedness to tangible net worth. At December 31, 2009, the Company was in compliance with all of these covenants. If the Company defaults on its payments, it is prohibited, subject to certain exceptions, from making dividend payments or other distributions. The Company also has available an unsecured and uncommitted revolving line of credit providing for borrowing to a maximum of $25,000,000. The revolving line accrues interest at LIBOR plus 125 basis points. There were no balances outstanding under either of these lines at December 31, 2009 and 2008.

The Company's Canadian subsidiary has available an unsecured and uncommitted line of credit guaranteed by the parent company providing for borrowing to a maximum of C$30,000,000 (US$28,485,000) at December 31, 2009. The revolving line accrues interest at the bank's Canadian prime rate. There was no balance outstanding under this line at December 31, 2009 and 2008.

The Company's European subsidiary has available two separate unsecured and uncommitted lines of credit guaranteed by the parent company providing for borrowing to a maximum of 30,000,000 and 20,000,000 euros respectively (combined US$71,602,000) at December 31, 2009, of which US$3,580,000 of the 20,000,000 euro line is designated as a European customs guarantee. These lines accrue interest based on the ECB refinancing rate plus 50 basis points and EONIA plus 75 basis points, respectively. There was no balance outstanding under either line at December 31, 2009 or 2008.

The Company's Japanese subsidiary has an unsecured and uncommitted line of credit guaranteed by the parent company providing for borrowing to a maximum of US$5,000,000 at December 31, 2009. The revolving line accrues interest at the bank's Best Lending Rate. There was no balance outstanding under this line at December 31, 2009 and 2008.

Off-Balance Sheet Arrangements

The Company has arrangements in place to facilitate the import and purchase of inventory through import letters of credit. The Company has available unsecured and uncommitted import letters of credit in the aggregate amount of $65,000,000 subject to annual renewal. At December 31, 2009, the Company had outstanding letters of credit of $7,771,000 for purchase orders for inventory under this arrangement.

Note 6 – Accrued Liabilities

Accrued liabilities consist of the following (in thousands):

	December 31,	
	2009	2008
Accrued salaries, bonus, vacation and other benefits	$ 34,711	$ 29,437
Accrued product warranty	12,112	9,746
Accrued cooperative advertising	4,358	6,457
Other	16,131	12,508
	$ 67,312	$ 58,148

Note 7 – Other Long-term Liabilities

Other long-term liabilities consist of deferred rent obligations, the effect of straight-line rent under various operating leases, rental asset retirement obligations, liabilities to participants in the Company's nonqualified deferred compensation plan, installment purchase obligations for non-inventory purchases made in the ordinary course of business and long-term severance liabilities. Deferred rent, straight-line rent, and rental asset retirement obligation liabilities were $14,218,000 and $10,126,000 at December 31, 2009 and 2008, respectively. The corresponding lease obligations for these deferred and straight-line rent liabilities are disclosed in Note 11. Principal payments due on other long-term liabilities are immaterial.

Note 8 – Shareholders' Equity

Since the inception of the Company's stock repurchase plan in 2004 through December 31, 2009, the Company's Board of Directors has authorized the repurchase of $500,000,000 of the Company's common stock. As of December 31, 2009, the Company has repurchased 8,897,957 shares under this program at an aggregate purchase price of approximately $407,399,000. During the year ended December 31, 2009, the Company repurchased an aggregate of $7,399,000 of the Company's common stock under the stock repurchase plan, of which $1,185,000 was recorded as a reduction to total retained earnings; otherwise, the aggregate purchase price would have resulted in a negative common stock carrying amount. Shares of the Company's common stock may be purchased in the open market or through privately negotiated transactions, subject to the market conditions. The repurchase program does not obligate the Company to acquire any specific number of shares or to acquire shares over any specified period of time.

Note 9 – Income Taxes

The Company applies an asset and liability method of accounting for income taxes that requires the recognition of deferred tax assets and liabilities for the expected future tax consequences of events that have been recognized in the Company's financial statements or tax returns. In estimating future tax consequences, the Company generally considers all expected future events other than enactment of changes in the tax laws or rates. Deferred taxes are provided for temporary differences between assets and liabilities for financial reporting purposes and for income tax purposes. Valuation allowances are recorded against net deferred tax assets when it is more likely than not that the asset will not be realized.

The Company had undistributed earnings of foreign subsidiaries of approximately $162,784,000 at December 31, 2009 for which deferred taxes have not been provided. Such earnings are considered indefinitely invested outside of the United States. If these earnings were repatriated to the United States, the earnings would be subject to U.S. taxation. The amount of the unrecognized deferred tax liability associated with the undistributed earnings was approximately $40,011,000 at December 31, 2009. The unrecognized deferred tax liability approximates the excess of the United States tax liability over the creditable foreign taxes paid that would result from a full remittance of undistributed earnings.

The Company recognizes the tax benefit from an uncertain tax position if it is more likely than not that the tax position will be sustained on examination by the relevant taxing authority based on the technical merits of the position. The tax benefits recognized in the financial statements from such positions are then measured based on the largest benefit that has a greater than 50% likelihood of being realized upon ultimate settlement with the relevant tax authority. In making this determination, the Company assumes that the taxing authority will examine the position and that they will have full knowledge of all relevant information. A reconciliation of the beginning and ending amount of gross unrecognized tax benefits is as follows (in thousands):

	December 31,	
	2009	2008
Balance at January 1	$ 21,839	$ 20,694
Increases related to prior years tax positions	1,346	583
Decreases related to prior years tax positions	(634)	(2,496)
Increases related to current year tax positions	1,598	4,768
Settlements	(1,194)	—
Lapses of statute of limitations	(2,772)	(1,710)
Balance at December 31	$ 20,183	$ 21,839

$18,659,000 and $20,096,000 of the unrecognized tax benefits balance would affect the effective tax rate if recognized at December 31, 2009 and 2008, respectively.

The Company conducts business globally, and as a result, the Company or one or more of its subsidiaries files income tax returns in the U.S. federal jurisdiction and various state and foreign jurisdictions. The Company is subject to examination by taxing authorities throughout the world, including such major jurisdictions as Canada, China, France, Germany, Hong Kong, Italy, Japan, South Korea, Switzerland, the United Kingdom and the United States. The Company has effectively settled U.S. tax examinations of all years through 2005. Internationally, the Company has effectively settled French tax examinations of all years through 2006 and Italian tax examinations of all years through 2007. The Company has effectively settled Canadian tax examinations of all years through 2004 and is currently under examination for the tax years 2005 through 2008. The Company does not anticipate that adjustments relative to this ongoing tax audit will result in a material change to its consolidated financial position, results of operations or cash flows.

Due to the potential for resolution of income tax audits currently in progress, and the expiration of various statutes of limitation, it is reasonably possible that the unrecognized tax benefits balance may change within the twelve months following December 31, 2009 by a range of zero to $9,181,000. At December 31, 2008, the comparable range was zero to $8,645,000. Open tax years, including those previously mentioned, contain matters that could be subject to differing interpretations of applicable tax laws and regulations as they relate to the amount, timing, or inclusion of revenue and expenses or the sustainability of income tax credits for a given examination cycle.

The Company recognizes interest expense and penalties related to income tax matters in income tax expense. The Company recognized a net reversal of accrued interest and penalties of $80,000 during 2009. The Company recognized net interest and penalties related to uncertain tax positions during 2008 of $313,000 and the Company recognized a net reversal of accrued interest and penalties of $117,000 during 2007. The Company had $3,155,000 and $3,234,000 of accrued interest and penalties related to uncertain tax positions at December 31, 2009 and 2008, respectively.

Consolidated income from continuing operations before income taxes consists of the following (in thousands):

	Year Ended December 31,		
	2009	2008	2007
U.S. operations	$ 59,629	$ 44,478	$ 122,588
Foreign operations	30,221	81,765	85,439
Income before income tax	$ 89,850	$ 126,243	$ 208,027

The components of the provision (benefit) for income taxes consist of the following (in thousands):

| | Year Ended December 31, | | |
	2009	2008	2007
Current:			
Federal	$ 10,030	$ 22,576	$ 40,490
State and local	2,088	2,459	3,685
Non-U.S.	10,399	18,568	22,493
	22,517	43,603	66,668
Deferred:			
Federal	2,377	(10,444)	(2,726)
State and local	12	(1,228)	(222)
Non-U.S.	(2,077)	(735)	(145)
	312	(12,407)	(3,093)
Income tax expense	$ 22,829	$ 31,196	$ 63,575

The following is a reconciliation of the normal expected statutory federal income tax rate to the effective rate reported in the financial statements:

| | Year Ended December 31, | | |
| | 2009 | 2008 | 2007 |
	(percent of income)		
Provision for federal income taxes at the statutory rate	35.0%	35.0%	35.0%
State and local income taxes, net of federal benefit	1.9	0.8	1.1
Non-U.S. income taxed at different rates	0.4	(4.1)	(1.4)
Foreign tax credits	(5.8)	(3.2)	—
Reduction of accrued income taxes	(4.1)	(3.3)	(2.8)
Tax-exempt interest	(0.5)	(0.8)	(1.0)
Other	(1.5)	0.3	(0.3)
Actual provision for income taxes	25.4%	24.7%	30.6%

Significant components of the Company's deferred taxes are as follows (in thousands):

| | December 31, | |
	2009	2008
Deferred tax assets:		
Non-deductible accruals and allowances	$ 18,979	$ 14,886
Capitalized inventory costs	15,326	14,703
Stock compensation	5,399	4,857
Net operating loss carryforward	4,734	2,130
Depreciation and amortization	582	972
Other	1,633	1,747
	46,653	39,295
Valuation allowance	(5,163)	(2,512)
Net deferred tax assets	41,490	36,783
Deferred tax liabilities:		
Deductible accruals and allowance	(1,129)	(1,396)
Depreciation and amortization	(4,624)	—
Foreign currency loss	(1,475)	(2,022)
Other	(1,368)	(744)
	(8,596)	(4,162)
Total	$ 32,894	$ 32,621

The Company had net operating loss carryforwards at December 31, 2009 and December 31, 2008 in certain international tax jurisdictions of $50,338,000 and $27,191,000, respectively which will begin to expire in 2014. The net operating losses result in a deferred tax asset at December 31, 2009 of $4,734,000, which was subject to a $4,734,000 valuation allowance, and a deferred tax asset at December 31, 2008 of $2,130,000, which was subject to a $2,130,000 valuation allowance. To the extent that the Company reverses a portion of the valuation allowance, the adjustment would be recorded as a reduction to income tax expense.

Non-current deferred tax assets of $5,435,000 and $723,000 are included as a component of other non-current assets in the consolidated balance sheet at December 31, 2009 and 2008, respectively.

Note 10 – Profit Sharing Plans

401(k) Profit-Sharing Plan

The Company has a 401(k) profit-sharing plan, which covers sub-stantially all U.S. employees. Participation begins the first of the quarter following completion of thirty days of service. The Company may elect to make discretionary matching and/or non-matching contributions. All Company contributions to the plan as deter-mined by the Board of Directors totaled $2,610,000, $3,118,000 and $5,083,000 for the years ended December 31, 2009, 2008 and 2007, respectively.

Deferred Compensation Plan

The Company sponsors a nonqualified retirement savings plan for certain senior management employees whose contributions to the tax qualified 401(k) plan would be limited by provisions of the Inter-nal Revenue Code. This plan allows participants to defer receipt of a portion of their salary and incentive compensation and to receive matching contributions for a portion of the deferred amounts. Com-pany contributions to the plan totaled $108,000 and $115,000 for the years ended December 31, 2009 and 2008, respectively. Partici-pants earn a return on their deferred compensation based on invest-ment earnings of participant-selected mutual funds. Changes in the market value of the participants' investment selections are recorded as an adjustment to deferred compensation liabilities, with an offset to compensation expense. Deferred compensation, including accu-mulated earnings on the participant-directed investment selections, is distributable in cash at participant-specified dates or upon retire-ment, death, disability or termination of employment. At December 31, 2009, the liability to participants under this plan was $826,000 and was recorded in other long-term liabilities. The current portion of the participant liability at December 31, 2009 was not material.

The Company has purchased specific mutual funds in the same amounts as the participant-directed investment selections underly-ing the deferred compensation liabilities. These investment securities and earnings thereon, held in an irrevocable trust, are intended to provide a source of funds to meet the deferred compensation obligations, subject to claims of creditors in the event of the Company's insolvency. The mutual funds are recorded at fair value in intangibles and other non-current assets. At December 31, 2009, the fair value of the mutual fund investments was $826,000. Realized and unrealized gains and losses on the mutual fund investments are recorded in compensation expense and offset losses and gains resulting from changes in deferred compensation liabilities to participants.

Note 11 – Commitments and Contingencies

Operating Leases

The Company leases, among other things, retail space, office space, warehouse facilities, storage space, vehicles and equipment. Generally, the base lease terms are between 5 and 10 years. Certain lease agreements contain scheduled rent escalation clauses in their future minimum lease payments. Future minimum lease payments are recognized on a straight-line basis over the minimum lease term and the pro rata portion of scheduled rent escalations is included in other long-term liabilities in the Consolidated Balance Sheet. Certain retail space lease agreements provide for additional rents based on a percentage of annual sales in excess of stipulated minimums (percentage rent). Certain lease agreements require the Company to pay real estate taxes, insurance, CAM, and other costs, collectively referred to as operating costs, in addition to base rent. Percentage rent and operating costs are recognized as incurred in SG&A expense in the Consolidated Statement of Operations. Certain lease agreements also contain lease incentives, such as tenant improvement allowances and rent holidays. The Company recognizes the benefits related to the lease incentives on a straight-line basis over the applicable lease term.

Rent expense, including percentage rent but excluding operating costs for which the Company is obligated, was $32,034,000, $25,220,000 and $13,938,000 for non-related party leases during the years ended December 31, 2009, 2008 and 2007, respectively. Of these amounts $30,569,000, $23,687,000 and $12,504,000 were included as part of selling, general and administrative expense for the years ended December 31, 2009, 2008 and 2007, respectively, and $1,465,000, $1,533,000 and $1,434,000 were included as part of cost of goods sold for the years ended December 31, 2009, 2008 and 2007, respectively.

The Company leases certain operating facilities from related parties of the Company. Total rent expense for these leases was included as part of selling, general and administrative expense and amounted to $571,000, $543,000 and $583,000 for the years ended December 31, 2009, 2008 and 2007, respectively.

Approximate future minimum payments, including rent escalation clauses and stores that are not yet open, on all lease obligations at December 31, 2009, are as follows (in thousands). Future minimum payments listed below do not include percentage rent or operating costs for which the Company is obligated.

	Non-related Parties	Related Party	Total
2010	$ 28,379	$ 625	$ 29,004
2011	27,534	625	28,159
2012	26,137	72	26,209
2013	25,678	72	25,750
2014	23,869	54	23,923
Thereafter	128,672	—	128,672
	$ 260,269	$ 1,448	$ 261,717

Inventory Purchase Obligations

Inventory purchase obligations consist of open production purchase orders for sourced apparel, footwear, accessories and equipment, and materials used to manufacture apparel. At December 31, 2009 and 2008 inventory purchase obligations were $258,069,000 and $157,774,000, respectively. To support certain inventory purchase obligations, the Company maintains unsecured and uncommitted lines of credit available for issuing import letters of credit. At

December 31, 2009, the Company had letters of credit of $7,771,000 outstanding for inventory purchase obligations. See *Off-Balance Sheet Arrangements* in Note 5 for further disclosure.

Litigation

The Company is a party to various legal claims, actions and complaints from time to time. Although the ultimate resolution of legal proceedings cannot be predicted with certainty, management believes that disposition of these matters will not have a material adverse effect on the Company's consolidated financial statements.

Indemnities and Guarantees

During its normal course of business, the Company has made certain indemnities, commitments and guarantees under which it may be required to make payments in relation to certain transactions. These include (i) intellectual property indemnities to the Company's customers and licensees in connection with the use, sale and/or license of Company products, (ii) indemnities to various lessors in connection with facility leases for certain claims arising from such facility or lease, (iii) indemnities to vendors and service providers pertaining to claims based on the negligence or willful misconduct of the Company, (iv) executive severance arrangements and (v) indemnities involving the accuracy of representations and warranties in certain contracts. The duration of these indemnities, commitments and guarantees varies, and in certain cases, may be indefinite. The majority of these indemnities, commitments and guarantees do not provide for any limitation of the maximum potential for future payments the Company could be obligated to make. The Company has not recorded any liability for these indemnities, commitments and guarantees in the accompanying Consolidated Balance Sheets.

Note 12 – Stock-based Compensation

The following table shows total stock-based compensation expense included in the Consolidated Statement of Operations for the years ended December 31, (in thousands):

	2009	2008	2007
Cost of sales	$ 335	$ 302	$ 415
Selling, general, and administrative expense	6,018	6,000	6,830
Licensing	—	—	15
Pre-tax stock-based compensation expense	6,353	6,302	7,260
Income tax benefits	(2,258)	(2,088)	(2,383)
Total stock-based compensation expense, net of tax	$ 4,095	$ 4,214	$ 4,877

No stock-based compensation costs were capitalized for the years ended December 31, 2009, 2008 and 2007.

The Company realized a tax benefit for the deduction from stock-based award transactions of $851,000, $636,000, and $4,213,000 for the years ended December 31, 2009, 2008 and 2007, respectively.

1997 Stock Incentive Plan

The Company's 1997 Stock Incentive Plan (the "Plan") provides for issuance of up to 8,900,000 shares of the Company's Common Stock, of which 2,106,182 shares were available for future grants under the Plan at December 31, 2009. The Plan allows for grants of incentive stock options, non-statutory stock options, restricted stock awards, restricted stock units and other stock-based awards. The Company uses original issuance shares to satisfy share-based payments.

Stock Options

Options to purchase the Company's common stock are granted at prices equal to or greater than the fair market value on the date of grant. Options granted prior to 2001 generally vested and became exercisable ratably on a monthly basis over a period of five years from the date of grant and expire ten years from the date of grant. Options granted after 2000 and before 2009 generally vest and become exercisable over a period of four years (twenty-five percent on the first anniversary date following the date of grant and monthly thereafter) and expire ten years from the date of the grant, with the exception of most options granted in 2005. Most options granted in 2005 vested and became exercisable one year from the date of grant and expire ten years from the date of grant. Options granted in 2009 generally vest and become exercisable ratably on an annual basis over a period of four years and expire ten years from the date of the grant.

The Company estimates the fair value of stock options using the Black-Scholes model. Key inputs and assumptions used to estimate the fair value of stock options include the exercise price of the award, the expected option term, the expected volatility of the Company's stock over the option's expected term, the risk-free interest rate over the option's expected term, and the Company's expected annual dividend yield. Assumptions are evaluated and revised as necessary to reflect changes in market conditions and the Company's experience. Estimates of fair value are not intended to predict actual future events or the value ultimately realized by people who receive equity awards.

The following table shows the weighted average assumptions for the year ended December 31:

	2009	2008	2007
Expected term	4.71 years	4.43 years	5.04 years
Expected stock price volatility	29.52%	25.03%	28.97%
Risk-free interest rate	1.73%	2.54%	4.55%
Expected dividend yield	2.17%	1.57%	1.01%
Weighted average grant date fair value	$ 6.55	$ 8.60	$ 18.87

The following table summarizes stock option activity under the Plan:

	Number of Shares	Weighted Average Exercise Price	Weighted Average Remaining Contractual Life	Aggregate Intrinsic Value (in thousands)
Options outstanding at January 1, 2007	1,579,150	$ 41.93	6.78	$ 21,761
Granted	263,272	61.44		

Cancelled	(81,160)	53.11		
Exercised	(402,845)	36.37		
Options outstanding at December 31, 2007	1,358,417	46.70	6.54	4,497
Granted	640,008	40.98		
Cancelled	(228,300)	49.49		
Exercised	(116,486)	32.42		
Options outstanding at December 31, 2008	1,653,639	45.10	6.73	1,042
Granted	387,505	29.75		
Cancelled	(252,303)	44.90		
Exercised	(28,668)	24.76		
Options outstanding at December 31, 2009	1,760,173	$ 42.08	6.25	$ 4,599
Options vested and expected to vest at December 31, 2009	1,707,304	$ 42.31	6.18	$ 4,289
Options exercisable at December 31, 2009	1,069,713	$ 45.56	4.94	$ 1,209

The aggregate intrinsic value in the table above represents pre-tax intrinsic value that would have been realized if all options had been exercised on the last business day of the period indicated, based on the Company's closing stock price on that day. Total stock option compensation expense for the years ended December 31, 2009, 2008 and 2007 was $2,861,000, $3,329,000 and $4,417,000, respectively. At December 31, 2009, 2008 and 2007, unrecognized costs related to stock options totaled approximately $4,609,000, $6,473,000 and $6,515,000, respectively, before any related tax benefit. The unrecognized costs related to stock options are being amortized over the related vesting period using the straight-line attribution method. Unrecognized costs related to stock options at December 31, 2009 are expected to be recognized over a weighted average period of 2.46 years. The aggregate intrinsic value of stock options exercised was $333,000, $1,071,000 and $10,953,000 for the years ended December 31, 2009, 2008 and 2007, respectively. The total cash received as a result of stock option exercises for the years ended December 31, 2009, 2008 and 2007 was $710,000, $3,731,000 and $14,604,000, respectively.

Restricted Stock Units

Service-based restricted stock units are granted at no cost to key employees and shares granted prior to 2009 generally vest over three years from the date of grant. Service-based restricted stock units granted in 2009 generally vest over a period of four years. Performance-based restricted stock units are granted at no cost to certain members of the Company's senior executive team, excluding the Chairman and the President and Chief Executive Officer, and generally vest over a performance period of between two and one-half and three years with an additional required service period of one year. Restricted stock units vest in accordance with the terms and conditions established by the Compensation Committee of the Board of Directors, and are based on continued service and, in some instances, on individual performance and/or Company performance. For the majority of restricted stock units granted, the number of shares issued on the date the restricted stock units vest is net of the minimum statutory withholding requirements that the Company pays in cash to the appropriate taxing authorities on behalf of its employees. For the years ended December 31, 2009, 2008 and 2007, the Company withheld 19,819, 5,951 and 7,176 shares, respectively, to satisfy $624,000, $243,000 and $442,000 of employees' tax obligations, respectively.

The fair value of service-based and performance-based restricted stock units is discounted by the present value of the estimated future stream of dividends over the vesting period using the Black-Scholes model. The relevant inputs and assumptions used in the Black-Scholes model to compute the discount are the vesting period, dividend yield and closing price of the Company's common stock on the date of grant.

The following table presents the weighted average assumptions for the years ended December 31:

	2009	2008	2007
Vesting period	3.82 years	3.06 years	3.11 years
Expected dividend yield	2.19%	1.56%	1.01%
Estimated average fair value per restricted stock unit granted	$ 27.14	$ 39.27	$ 60.16

The following table summarizes the restricted stock unit activity under the Plan:

	Number of Shares	Weighted Average Grant Date Fair Value Per Share
Restricted stock units outstanding at January 1, 2007	99,688	$ 49.06
Granted	98,422	60.16
Vested	(21,622)	49.79
Forfeited	(16,618)	53.72
Restricted stock units outstanding at December 31, 2007	159,870	55.31
Granted	168,347	39.27
Vested	(20,625)	51.85
Forfeited	(47,083)	49.25
Restricted stock units outstanding at December 31, 2008	260,509	46.32
Granted	136,327	27.14
Vested	(65,935)	53.41
Forfeited	(44,381)	41.22
Restricted stock units outstanding at December 31, 2009	286,520	$ 36.35

Restricted stock unit compensation expense for the years ended December 31, 2009, 2008 and 2007 was $3,492,000, $2,973,000 and $2,843,000, respectively. At December 31, 2009, 2008 and 2007, unrecognized costs related to restricted stock units totaled approximately $4,216,000, $5,499,000 and $5,963,000, respectively, before any related tax benefit. The unrecognized costs related to restricted stock units are being amortized over the related vesting period using the straight-line attribution method. These unrecognized costs at December 31, 2009 are expected to be recognized over a weighted average period of 1.95 years. The total grant date fair value of restricted stock units vested during the year ended December 31, 2009, 2008 and 2007 was $3,522,000, $1,069,000 and $1,077,000, respectively.

1999 Employee Stock Purchase Plan

In 1999, the Company's shareholders approved the 1999 Employee Stock Purchase Plan ("ESPP"). There are 750,000 shares of common stock authorized for issuance under the ESPP, which allows qualified employees of the Company to purchase shares on a quarterly basis up to fifteen percent of their respective compensation. The purchase price of the shares is equal to eighty five percent of the lesser of the closing price of the Company's common stock on the first or last trading day of the respective quarter. Effective July 1, 2005, the Company suspended offerings under the ESPP indefinitely. As of December 31, 2009, a total of 275,556 shares of common stock had been issued under the ESPP.

Note 13 – Earnings Per Share

Earnings per Share ("EPS"), is presented on both a basic and diluted basis. Basic EPS is based on the weighted average number of common shares outstanding. Diluted EPS reflects the potential dilution that could occur if outstanding securities or other contracts to issue common stock were exercised or converted into common stock. For the calculation of diluted EPS, the basic weighted average number of shares is increased by the dilutive effect of stock options and restricted stock units determined using the treasury stock method.

A reconciliation of the common shares used in the denominator for computing basic and diluted EPS is as follows (in thousands, except per share amounts):

| | Year Ended December 31, | | |
	2009	2008	2007
Weighted average common shares outstanding, used in computing basic earnings per share	33,846	34,610	36,106
Effect of dilutive stock options and restricted stock units	135	101	328
Weighted-average common shares outstanding, used in computing diluted earnings per share	33,981	34,711	36,434
Earnings per share of common stock:			
Basic	$ 1.98	$ 2.75	$ 4.00
Diluted	1.97	2.74	3.96

Stock options and service-based restricted stock units representing 1,562,064, 1,410,849 and 354,342 shares of common stock for the years ended December 31, 2009, 2008 and 2007, respectively, were outstanding but were excluded in the computation of diluted EPS because their effect would be anti-dilutive as a result of applying the treasury stock method. In addition, performance-based restricted stock units representing 44,043, 41,799 and 24,318 shares for the years ended December 31, 2009, 2008 and 2007, respectively, were outstanding but were excluded from the computation of diluted EPS because these shares were subject to performance conditions that had not been met.

Since the inception of the Company's stock repurchase plan in 2004 through December 31, 2009, the Company's Board of Directors has authorized the repurchase of $500,000,000 of the Company's common stock.

As of December 31, 2009, the Company has repurchased 8,897,957 shares under this program at an aggregate purchase price of approximately $407,399,000. During the year ended December 31, 2009, the Company repurchased an aggregate of $7,399,000 of the Company's common stock under the stock repurchase plan, of which $1,185,000 was recorded as a reduction to total retained earnings; otherwise, the aggregate purchase price would have resulted in a negative common stock carrying amount. Shares of the Company's common stock may be purchased in the open market or through privately negotiated transactions, subject to the market conditions. The repurchase program does not obligate the Company to acquire any specific number of shares or to acquire shares over any specified period of time.

Note 14 – Comprehensive Income

Accumulated other comprehensive income, net of applicable taxes, reported on the Company's Consolidated Balance Sheets consists of foreign currency translation adjustments, unrealized gains and losses on derivative transactions and unrealized gains on available-for-sale securities. A summary of comprehensive income, net of related tax effects, for the year ended December 31, is as follows (in thousands):

	2009	2008	2007
Net income	$ 67,021	$ 95,047	$ 144,452
Other comprehensive income (loss):			
Unrealized holding gains on available-for-sale securities	64	—	—
Unrealized derivative holding gains (losses) arising during period (net of tax expense (benefit) of, ($1,054) $361 and ($796) in 2009, 2008 and 2007, respectively)	(3,024)	6,425	(844)
Reclassification to net income of previously deferred gains on derivative transactions (net of tax benefit of $227, $36 and $608 in 2009, 2008 and 2007, respectively)	(616)	(389)	(1,303)
Foreign currency translation adjustments	13,854	(30,511)	25,394
Other comprehensive income (loss)	10,278	(24,475)	23,247
Comprehensive income	$ 77,299	$ 70,572	$ 167,699

Note 15 – Segment Information

The Company operates in four geographic segments: (1) United States, (2) Europe, Middle East and Africa ("EMEA"), (3) Latin America and Asia Pacific ("LAAP"), and (4) Canada, which are reflective of the Company's internal organization, management, and oversight structure. Each geographic segment operates predominantly in one industry: the design, development, marketing and distribution of active outdoor apparel, including sportswear, outerwear, footwear, accessories and equipment.

The geographic distribution of the Company's net sales, income before income taxes, interest income (expense), income tax expense (benefit), depreciation and amortization expense and identifiable assets are summarized in the following tables (in thousands) for, and for the years ended, December 31, 2009, 2008 and 2007. Inter-geographic net sales, which are recorded at a negotiated mark-up and eliminated in consolidation, are not material.

	2009	2008	2007
Net sales to unrelated entities:			
United States	$ 736,942	$ 727,706	$ 767,198
EMEA	197,357	267,152	286,968
LAAP	203,230	198,236	175,725
Canada	106,494	124,741	126,148
	$ 1,244,023	$ 1,317,835	$ 1,356,039
Income before income taxes:			
United States	$ 49,660	$ 38,674	$ 112,986
EMEA	1,410	26,167	29,210
LAAP	27,138	32,857	29,585
Canada	9,554	21,008	27,195
Interest and other income and eliminations	2,088	7,537	9,051
	$ 89,850	$ 126,243	$ 208,027
Interest income (expense), net:			
United States	$ 4,561	$ 5,804	$ 9,602
EMEA	(910)	45	(1,856)
LAAP	561	1,023	482
Canada	(2,124)	665	660
	$ 2,088	$ 7,537	$ 8,888

Income tax (expense) benefit:

United States	$ (13,710)	$ (13,363)	$ (41,227)
EMEA	(2,744)	(2,692)	(5,185)
LAAP	(6,745)	(8,312)	(7,084)
Canada	370	(6,829)	(10,079)
	$ (22,829)	$ (31,196)	$ (63,575)

Depreciation and amortization expense:

United States	$ 26,850	$ 21,866	$ 18,643
EMEA	6,642	6,978	9,910
LAAP	2,120	1,865	1,540
Canada	641	449	245
	$ 36,253	$ 31,158	$ 30,338

	2009	2008	2007
Assets:			
United States	$ 916,847	$ 857,228	$ 8 72,027
EMEA	249,838	246,072	239,007
LAAP	104,734	93,773	78,308
Canada	127,205	89,463	97,815
Total identifiable assets	1,398,624	1,286,536	1,287,157
Eliminations and reclassifications	(185,741)	(138,300)	(120,676)
Total assets	$ 1,212,883	$ 1,148,236	$ 1,166,481
Net sales to unrelated entities:			
Sportswear	$ 472,508	$ 540,903	$ 565,591
Outerwear	482,512	491,777	497,551
Footwear	214,565	217,237	227,434
Accessories and equipment	74,438	67,918	65,463
	$ 1,244,023	$ 1,317,835	$ 1,356,039

Note 16 – Financial Instruments and Risk Management

In the normal course of business, the Company's financial position and results of operations are routinely subject to a variety of risks, including market risk associated with interest rate movements on borrowings and investments and currency rate movements on non-functional currency denominated assets, liabilities and income. The Company regularly assesses these risks and has established policies and business practices that serve to mitigate these potential exposures. As part of the Company's risk management programs, the Company may use a variety of financial instruments, including foreign currency option and forward contracts. The Company does not hold or issue derivative financial instruments for trading or speculative purposes.

The Company's foreign currency risk management objective is to mitigate the uncertainty of anticipated cash flows attributable to changes in exchange rates. Particular focus is put on cash flows resulting from anticipated inventory purchases and the related receivables and payables, including third party or intercompany transactions. The Company manages this risk primarily by using currency forward exchange contracts and options. Anticipated transactions that are hedged carry a high level of certainty and are expected to be recognized within one year. In addition, the Company may use cross-currency swaps to hedge foreign currency denominated payments related to intercompany loan agreements.

The Company hedges against the exchange rate risk associated with anticipated transactions denominated in non-functional currencies and accounts for these instruments as cash flow hedges. The effective change in fair value of these financial instruments is initially offset to accumulated other comprehensive income and any ineffective portion offset to current income. Amounts accumulated in other comprehensive income are subsequently reclassified to cost of sales when the underlying transaction is included in income. Hedge effectiveness is determined by evaluating the ability of a hedging instrument's cumulative change in fair value to offset the cumulative change in the present value of expected cash flows on the underlying exposures. For forward contracts and options, the change in fair value attributable to changes in forward points and time value, respectively, are excluded from the determination of hedge effectiveness and included in current cost of sales. Hedge ineffectiveness was not material during the years ended December 31, 2009, 2008 and 2007. The Company did not discontinue any material cash flow hedging relationships during the years ended December 31, 2009, 2008 and 2007 because it remained probable that the forecasted transactions would occur by the end of the specified period.

At December 31, 2009, the notional value of outstanding forward contracts designated as hedging anticipated inventory purchases was approximately $82,730,000. At December 31, 2009, insignificant deferred gains and losses (net of tax) on both outstanding and matured derivatives accumulated in other comprehensive income are expected to be reclassified to net income during the next twelve months as a result of underlying hedged transactions also being recorded in net income. Actual amounts ultimately reclassified to net income are dependent on U.S. dollar exchange rates in effect against the European euro, Canadian dollar, Japanese yen and Korean won when outstanding derivative contracts mature.

The classification of effective hedge results in the Consolidated Statements of Operations is the same as that of the underlying exposure. Results of hedges of product costs are recorded in cost of sales when the underlying hedged transaction affects income. Unrealized derivative gains and losses, which are recorded in current assets and liabilities, respectively, are non-cash items and therefore are taken into account in the preparation of the Consolidated Statements of Cash Flows based on their respective balance sheet classifications.

The Company also uses derivative instruments not formally designated as hedges to manage the exchange rate risk associated with the functional currency remeasurement of monetary assets and liabilities. At December 31, 2009, the notional value of outstanding forward contracts not formally designated as hedges was approximately $61,017,000. The change in fair value of these instruments is recognized immediately in cost of sales.

The Company does not hold derivatives featuring credit-related contingent terms. In addition, the Company is not a party to any derivative master agreement featuring credit-related contingent terms. Finally, the Company has not pledged assets or posted collateral as a requirement for entering into or maintaining derivative positions. See "Concentration of credit risk" under Note 1 for more information on credit risk related to financial instruments.

The following table presents the balance sheet classification and fair value of derivative instruments as of December 31, 2009 (in thousands):

	Classification	Fair Value
Derivative instruments designated as cash flow hedges(1):		
Derivative instruments in asset positions:		
Currency forward contracts	Prepaid expenses and other current assets	$ 1,099
Derivative instruments in liability positions:		
Currency forward contracts	Accrued liabilities	890

(1) Includes a $45,000 net liability position attributable to the component excluded from effectiveness testing.

	Classification	Fair Value
Derivative instruments not designated as hedges:		
Derivative instruments in asset positions:		
Currency forward contracts	Prepaid expenses and other current assets	$ 453
Derivative instruments in liability positions:		
Currency forward contracts	Accrued liabilities	1,065

The following table presents the effect and classification of derivative instruments for the year ended December 31, 2009 (in thousands):

	Statement of Operations Classification	Gain (loss)
Currency Forward Contracts:		
Derivative instruments designated as cash flow hedges:		
Loss recognized in other comprehensive income, net of tax	—	$ (3,024)
Loss reclassified from accumulated other comprehensive income to income for the effective portion, net of tax	Cost of sales	(740)
Loss recognized in income for amount excluded from effectiveness testing and for the ineffective portion(1)	Cost of sales	(14)
Derivative instruments not designated as cash flow hedges:		
Loss recognized in income	Cost of sales	(130)

(1) During the periods presented, the Company recognized an immaterial amount of ineffectiveness.

Note 17 – Fair Value Measures

Certain assets and liabilities are reported at fair value on either a recurring or nonrecurring basis. Fair value is defined as an exit price, representing the amount that would be received to sell an asset or paid to transfer a liability in an orderly transaction between market participants, under a three-tier fair value hierarchy which prioritizes the inputs used in measuring fair value as follows:

Level 1 –   observable inputs such as quoted prices in active markets;
Level 2 –   inputs, other than the quoted market prices in active markets, which are observable, either directly or indirectly; and
Level 3 –   unobservable inputs for which there is little or no market data available, which require the reporting entity to develop its own assumptions.

Assets and liabilities measured at fair value on a recurring basis as of December 31, 2009 are as follows (in thousands):

	Total	Level 1 (1)	Level 2 (2)	Level 3
Assets:				
Cash and cash equivalents	$ 386,664	$ 386,664	$ —	$ —
Short-term investments	22,759	22,759	—	—
Long-term investments	826	826	—	—
Derivative financial instruments	1,552	—	1,552	—
Liabilities:				
Derivative financial instruments	1,955	—	1,955	—

(1) Level 1 assets include cash equivalents consisting of money market funds, ultra-short bond funds, bank deposits and time deposits for which cost approximates fair value and long-term investments consisting of equity-concentrated mutual funds held to offset deferred compensation arrangements.
(2) Level 2 assets and liabilities include derivative financial instruments which are valued based on significant observable inputs. See Note 14 and Note 16 for further discussion.

There were no assets and liabilities measured at fair value on a nonrecurring basis.

SUPPLEMENTARY DATA – QUARTERLY FINANCIAL DATA (Unaudited)

The following table summarizes the Company's quarterly financial data for the past two years ended December 31, 2009 (in thousands, except per share amounts):

2009	First Quarter	Second Quarter	Third Quarter	Fourth Quarter
Net sales	$ 271,966	$ 179,268	$ 434,473	$ 358,316
Gross profit	110,495	74,307	188,599	150,677
Net income (loss)	6,898	(9,878)	46,915	23,086
Earnings (loss) per share				
Basic	$ 0.20	$ (0.29)	$ 1.39	$ 0.68
Diluted	0.20	(0.29)	1.38	0.68

2008	First Quarter	Second Quarter	Third Quarter	Fourth Quarter
Net sales	$ 297,363	$ 213,147	$ 452,415	$ 354,910
Gross profit	130,555	85,765	202,053	149,438
Net income (loss)	19,931	(1,770)	58,329	18,557
Earnings (loss) per share				
Basic	$ 0.56	$ (0.05)	$ 1.70	$ 0.55
Diluted	0.56	(0.05)	1.69	0.55

Item 9. *CHANGES IN AND DISAGREEMENTS WITH ACCOUNTANTS ON ACCOUNTING AND FINANCIAL DISCLOSURE*

None.

Item 9A. *CONTROLS AND PROCEDURES*

Evaluation of Disclosure Controls and Procedures

Our management has evaluated, under the supervision and with the participation of our chief executive officer and chief financial officer, the effectiveness of our disclosure controls and procedures as of the end of the period covered by this report pursuant to Rule 13a-15(b) under the Securities Exchange Act of 1934 (the "Exchange Act"). Based on that evaluation, our chief executive officer and chief financial officer have concluded that, as of the end of the period covered by this report, our disclosure controls and procedures are effective in ensuring that information required to be disclosed in our Exchange Act reports is (1) recorded, processed, summarized and reported in a timely manner, and (2) accumulated and communicated to our management, including our chief executive officer and chief financial officer, as appropriate to allow timely decisions regarding required disclosure.

Design and Evaluation of Internal Control Over Financial Reporting

Report of Management

Our management is responsible for establishing and maintaining adequate internal control over financial reporting. All internal control systems, no matter how well designed, have inherent limitations. Therefore, even those systems determined to be effective can provide only reasonable assurance with respect to financial statement preparation and presentation.

Under the supervision and with the participation of our management, we assessed the effectiveness of our internal control over financial reporting as of December 31, 2009. In making this assessment, we used the criteria set forth by the Committee of Sponsoring Organizations of the Treadway Commission in Internal Control – Integrated Framework. Based on our assessment we believe that, as of December 31, 2009, the Company's internal control over financial reporting is effective based on those criteria.

There has been no change in our internal control over financial reporting that occurred during our fiscal quarter ended December 31, 2009 that has materially affected, or is reasonably likely to materially affect, our internal control over financial reporting.

Our independent auditors have issued an audit report on the effectiveness of our internal control over financial reporting as of December 31, 2009, which is included herein.

Report of Independent Registered Public Accounting Firm

To the Board of Directors and Shareholders
Columbia Sportswear Company
Portland, Oregon

We have audited the internal control over financial reporting of Columbia Sportswear Company and subsidiaries (the "Company") as of December 31, 2009, based on criteria established in *Internal Control – Integrated Framework* issued by the Committee of Sponsoring Organizations of the Treadway Commission. The Company's management is responsible for maintaining effective internal control over financial reporting and for its assessment of the effectiveness of internal control over financial reporting, included in the accompanying "Report of Management". Our responsibility is to express an opinion on the Company's internal control over financial reporting based on our audit.

We conducted our audit in accordance with the standards of the Public Company Accounting Oversight Board (United States). Those standards require that we plan and perform the audit to obtain reasonable assurance about whether effective internal control over financial reporting was maintained in all material respects. Our audit included obtaining an understanding of internal control over financial reporting, assessing the risk that a material weakness exists, testing and evaluating the design and operating effectiveness of internal control based on the assessed risk, and performing such other procedures as we considered necessary in the circumstances. We believe that our audit provides a reasonable basis for our opinion.

A company's internal control over financial reporting is a process designed by, or under the supervision of, the company's principal executive and principal financial officers, or persons performing similar functions, and effected by the company's board of directors, management, and other personnel to provide reasonable assurance regarding the reliability of financial reporting and the preparation of financial statements for external purposes in accordance with generally accepted accounting principles. A company's internal control over financial reporting includes those policies and procedures that (1) pertain to the maintenance of records that, in reasonable detail, accurately and fairly reflect the transactions and dispositions of the assets of the company; (2) provide reasonable assurance that transactions are recorded as necessary to permit preparation of financial statements in accordance with generally accepted accounting principles, and that receipts and expenditures of the company are being made only in accordance with authorizations of management and directors of the company; and (3) provide reasonable assurance regarding prevention or timely detection of unauthorized acquisition, use, or disposition of the company's assets that could have a material effect on the financial statements.

Because of the inherent limitations of internal control over financial reporting, including the possibility of collusion or improper management override of controls, material misstatements due to error or fraud may not be prevented or detected on a timely basis. Also, projections of any evaluation of the effectiveness of the internal control over financial reporting to future periods are subject to the risk that the controls may become inadequate because of changes in conditions, or that the degree of compliance with the policies or procedures may deteriorate.

In our opinion, the Company maintained, in all material respects, effective internal control over financial reporting as of December 31, 2009, based on the criteria established in *Internal Control – Integrated Framework* issued by the Committee of Sponsoring Organizations of the Treadway Commission.

We have also audited, in accordance with the standards of the Public Company Accounting Oversight Board (United States), the consolidated financial statements and financial statement schedule as of and for the year ended December 31, 2009 of the Company and our report dated March 12, 2010 expressed an unqualified opinion on those financial statements and financial statement schedule.

DELOITTE & TOUCHE LLP
Portland, Oregon
March 12, 2010

APPENDIX B

GLOSSARY

Accelerated depreciation. A method of calculating depreciation which results in the charges becoming progressively smaller each period.

Account. An account is a device for accumulating additions and subtractions of a single asset, liability or owners' equity item, including revenues and expenses.

Accounting. A system to convey financial information about a specific entity. AICPA defines accounting as a service activity whose "function is to provide quantitative information, primarily financial in nature, about economic entities that is intended to be useful in making economic decisions."

Accounting entity. A person, partnership, corporation or other organization operating as a single economic entity.

Accounting equation. Assets + Equities; Assets = Liabilities + Owners' Equity.

Accounting principles. The methods or procedures used in accounting for events reported in the financial statements and which have received official authoritative sanction from FASB or the SEC.

Accounts payable. A liability representing an amount owed to a creditor; usually arising from the purchase of merchandise or materials and supplies; normally, a current liability.

Accounts receivable. Claims against a debtor; usually arising from sales or services rendered.

Accounts receivable turnover. Net sales divided by average accounts receivable.

Accrual basis of accounting. The method of recognizing revenues when a firm sells goods (or delivers them) or renders services and recognizing expenses when they are incurred.

Accumulated depreciation. A contra account which shows the sum of depreciation charges on an asset since the time the firm placed it in service.

Acid test ratio. Quick assets divided by total current liabilities.

Activity-based costing (ABC). A method of assigning overhead costs to products and services. ABC assumes that overhead costs are related to the production activities of the firm and vary with respect to the drivers of those activities. This method assigns costs first to activities and then to products based on the products' usage of the activities.

Activity-based management (ABM). Analysis and management of activities required to make a product or to produce a service. ABM focuses attention to enhance activities that add value to the customer and to reduce activities that do not. Its goal is to satisfy customer needs while making smaller demands on costly resources. Some refer to this as "activity management."

Additional paid-in capital. An alternative acceptable title for the capital contributed in excess of par (or stated) value account.

Adjunct account. An account that accompanies and increases another account, as opposed to a contra account which accompanies and reduces another account.

Adjusting entry. An entry made at the end of an accounting period to update an account.

Adverse opinion. An auditor's report stating that an organization's financial statements are not fair or are not in accord with GAAP.

Allocate. To divide or spread a cost or revenue item from one account into two or more cost objects. Allocation is, by nature, arbitrary. (See *Arbitrary* below.)

Allocation base. The systematic method that assigns joint costs to cost objectives.

Allowance for uncollectibles (accounts receivable). A contra account that shows the estimated accounts receivable amount that the firm expects not to collect.

Amortization. Process of allocating the acquisition cost of an asset either to the periods of benefit as an expense or to inventory accounts as a product cost.

Annual report. A report prepared once a year for shareholders and other interested parties. It includes a balance sheet, an income statement, a statement of cash flows, a reconciliation of changes in owners' equity accounts, a summary of significant accounting principles, other explanatory notes, the auditor's report, and comments from management about the year's events.

Applied cost. A cost that a firm has allocated to a department, product or activity; not necessarily based on actual costs incurred.

Arbitrary. Having no causation basis.

Asset. A resource which provides a future economic benefit *to its owner*.

Audit. A systematic inspection of accounting records involving analyses, tests and confirmations.

Audit committee. A committee of the board of directors of an organization who engage the independent auditors and discuss the auditors' work with them.

Auditing standards. Standards promulgated by the PCAOB for auditors to follow in carrying out their attest functions.

Auditor's report. The auditor's statement of the work done and an opinion of the financial statements of an organization.

Balance sheet. Also known as the statement of financial position. It is based on the equation Total Assets = Total Liabilities + Owners' Equity.

Balance sheet account. An account that appears on a balance sheet. These are often referred to as "permanent accounts."

Balanced scorecard. A set of performance targets, some of which are not financial, that are designed to further an organization's strategic plan.

Basic earnings per share. Net income minus preferred dividends, divided by the weighted average number of common shares outstanding during the period.

Board of directors. The governing body of a corporation; elected by the shareholders.

Bond. A certificate showing evidence of debt and containing the conditions such as the interest rate, maturity date and face amount of the debt. Normally, bonds call for semiannual payments.

Book value. The amount shown in the books or in the accounts for an asset, liability or owners' equity item. For depreciable assets, book value is the cost of the asset less accumulated depreciation.

Book value per share of common stock. Common shareholders' equity divided by the number of shares of common stock outstanding.

Bookkeeping. The process of analyzing and recording transactions in the accounting records.

Breakeven point. The volume of sales required so that total revenues equal total costs.

Budget. A financial plan that a firm develops to plan and control operations.

Budgeted statements. Pro forma financial statements prepared beforehand.

Callable bond. A bond which allows the issuer to retire (call) the bond at a specific amount before its maturity date.

Capital. The owners' equity in a business.

Capital budget. Plan of proposed outlays for acquiring long-term assets and the means of financing the acquisition.

Capital budgeting. The process of choosing large-scale projects for an organization. This generally requires estimating the present value of cash flows associated with the project.

Capital contributed in excess of par (or stated) value. The amount received when a corporation issues capital stock for an amount greater than its par (or stated) value.

Capital gain. The excess of proceeds over cost, or other basis, from the sale of a capital asset.

Capital lease. A lease treated by the lessee as both the borrowing of funds and the acquisition of an asset to be amortized. The lessee (tenant) recognizes both the liability and the asset on its balance sheet. Expenses consist of interest on the debt and amortization of the asset. The lessor (landlord) treats the lease as the sale of the asset in return for a series of future cash receipts. Contrast with operating lease.

Capital stock. The ownership shares of a corporation.

Capitalize. Recording an expenditure as an asset rather than an expense.

Cash. Currency and coins, negotiable checks, and balances in bank accounts. For the statement of cash flows, "cash" also includes marketable securities held as current assets.

Cash basis of accounting. A method of accounting in which a firm recognizes revenues when it receives cash and recognizes expenses when it makes a payment.

Cash provided by operations. A subsection of the cash flow statement. It is calculated as net income plus expenses not requiring cash plus increases in current liabilities and decreases in current assets, less increases in current assets and reductions in current liabilities.

Common cost. A cost attributable to two or more cost objects.

These costs are then allocated between the cost objects (products, services, departments or time periods) which benefit from the incurrence of the cost.

Common shares. The ultimate claim to the residual rights to a corporation's earnings and assets after the firm has met all debt and preferred shareholders' claims.

Comparative (financial) statements. Financial statements showing information for the same company for different periods.

Compound interest. Interest calculated on principal plus previously earned interest.

Conservatism. An accounting convention which calls for the anticipation of losses and expenses but defers recognition of gains or profits until they are realized in arm's-length transactions.

Consistency. An accounting convention which requires similar transactions be treated in the same way in consecutive periods in order for financial statements to be comparable.

Consolidated financial statements. Statements that are issued by legally separate companies and that show financial position and income as they would appear if the companies were one economic entity.

Contra account. An account, such as accumulated depreciation, which reduces the book value of another account, such as buildings and machinery.

Contributed capital. The owners' equity account that represents a firm's capital paid in by the owners.

Contribution margin. Revenues less all variable expenses.

Contribution margin ratio. Contribution margin divided by net sales.

Convertible bond. A bond whose owner may convert it into a specified number of shares of capital stock during the conversion period.

Corporation. A legal entity authorized by a state to operate under the rules of the entity's charter.

Cost. The amount of assets given up or the liability incurred in order to acquire some good or service.

Cost accounting. Classifying, summarizing, recording, reporting and allocating current or predicted costs.

Cost allocation. Assigning costs to individual cost objects.

Cost behavior. The relation between changes in a cost driver and changes in cost. Costs can be classified as variable, fixed or mixed.

Cost/benefit approach. An approach to decision making and resource allocation which compares some measure of benefits with the expected costs for a proposed undertaking.

Cost driver. A factor that causes an activity's costs.

Cost of capital. The rate of return owners require an investment to earn.

Cost of goods manufactured. The cost of direct materials, labor and overhead allocated to products completed during a period.

Cost of goods sold. The cost of beginning inventory plus cost of goods purchased or manufactured minus ending inventory equals a firm's cost of goods sold during a period of time.

Cost pool. A grouping of similar costs.

Cost-volume-profit analysis. A study of the sensitivity of costs and profits to changes in the amount of sales.

Current assets. Cash and other assets that a firm expects to turn into cash, sell or exchange within the normal operating cycle of the firm or one year, whichever is longer.

Current liability. A debt or other obligation that a firm must discharge within an operating cycle by expending current assets.

Current ratio. Current assets divided by current liabilities.

Debit. Debit does not mean increase or decrease. It is simply an entry on the left-hand side of an account.

Debt. An amount owed. The general name for notes, bonds, mortgages and the like that provide evidence of amounts owed and have definite payment dates.

Debt/equity ratio. Total liabilities divided by total equities.

Debt-financing. Raising funds by borrowing.

Depreciable cost. That part of the cost of an asset, usually acquisition cost less salvage value, that the firm will charge off over the life of the asset through the process of depreciation.

Depreciation. The process of allocating the cost of an asset to the periods of benefit over the life of the asset.

Differential analysis. Analysis of differential outcomes from two or more alternatives.

Direct cost. A cost which can be traced directly to a given cost object. The cost of materials can often be traced directly to a product. An employee's salary can be traced directly to the department in which she works.

Dividend yield. Dividends declared for the year divided by market price of the stock.

Earnings per share (of common stock). Net income attributable to common shareholders (net income minus preferred dividends) divided by the weighted average number of common shares outstanding.

EBIT. Earnings before interest and income taxes.

Economic order quantity (EOQ). A decision model which calculates the optimal quantity of inventory to order under a set of assumptions.

Efficient capital market. A market in which security prices reflect all publicly available information and react nearly instantaneously in an unbiased manner to information.

Expense. The outflows of cash, the decreases in other assets or the incurrence of liabilities resulting from the performance of activities that constitute an organization's principal operations.

Extraordinary item. A material expense or revenue item that is both unusual and infrequent.

FASB (Financial Accounting Standards Board). An independent board responsible for establishing generally accepted accounting principles.

FIFO (first-in-first-out). An inventory cost-flow assumption that firms use to compute ending inventory cost and cost of goods sold. It assumes sales are made from the oldest purchases.

Financial accounting. Focuses on reporting to external parties such as investors and creditors.

Financial statements. The balance sheet, income statement, statement of retained earnings, statement of cash flows, statement of changes in owners' equity accounts, statement of comprehensive income, and notes thereto.

Flexible budget. Budget based on standard inputs per unit and actual output.

Footnotes. Detailed information accompanying the financial statements.

GAAP. Generally accepted accounting principles.

Gain. The increase in owners' equity caused by an event that is not part of a firm's normal operations.

General journal. The formal record in which the firm records transactions, or summaries of similar transactions, in journal entry form as they occur.

General ledger. The name for the formal ledger containing all the financial statement accounts.

Goal congruence. Goal congruence exists when employees working in their own enlightened self-interest take actions that align with organizational goals.

Going-concern assumption. The assumption that a business will remain in operation indefinitely.

Goodwill. The excess of cost of an acquired firm over the current fair market value of its separately identifiable net assets.

Gross margin. Net sales minus cost of goods sold.

Historical cost. Acquisition cost.

Hurdle rate. Required rate of return in a discounted cash flow analysis.

Income. Excess of revenues and gains over expenses and losses for a period.

Income statement. The statement of revenues, expenses, gains and losses for a period of time.

Indirect costs. Costs not easily traceable to specific cost objects.

Insolvent. Unable to pay one's debts.

Internal rate of return (IRR). The discount rate that equates the net present values of a stream of cash outflows and inflows to zero.

Inventory turnover. Number of times the firm sells the average inventory during a period; cost of goods sold for a period divided by average inventory for the period.

Joint costs. Common costs incurred in the simultaneous production of two or more products.

Just-in-time inventory system. An inventory system that

purchases or produces goods and materials only as needed and just in time to be used at each stage of the production process.

Kaizen costing. A Japanese management approach which seeks incremental, continuous improvements.

Liability. An obligation to transfer assets or provide services to another entity.

LIFO (last-in-first-out). An inventory valuation method which assumes the cost of goods sold equals the cost of the most recently acquired units, and a firm computes the ending inventory cost from the costs of the oldest units.

Liquid assets. Cash, marketable securities and current receivables.

Liquidity. The ability of a firm to pay current obligations.

Long-term, long-run. An ambiguous term. Generally speaking, the long-term occurs when a firm is able to increase its productive capacity. For some firms this may be weeks or months; for other firms this may be years.

Management by exception. A management practice in which managers focus attention on areas not performing as expected and give less attention to areas operating as expected.

Managerial accounting. Accounting systems designed to provide managers with information needed for planning, organizing, controlling and decision making.

Margin of safety. Amount by which actual sales exceed breakeven sales.

Marginal cost. The additional cost of an additional unit produced or purchased.

Marginal revenue. The additional revenue from the sale an additional unit of product.

Net assets. Total assets minus total liabilities, also the amount of owners' equity.

Net current assets. Current assets minus current liabilities.

Net operating profit. Income from continuing operations.

Net present value. The value today of a net future cash flow (inflow less outflow) discounted at a given rate of interest.

Net sales. Total sales less sales returns, allowances and discounts.

Objectivity. The accounting principle of not recording an event until events can be measured with reasonable accuracy and independently verified.

Operating budget. A pro forma income statement, balance sheet and their supporting schedules.

Operating expenses. Expenses incurred in carrying out the ordinary activities of an organization.

Operating leverage. The tendency of net income to rise or fall at a faster rate than sales in the presence of fixed costs. The greater the fixed costs vis-à-vis variable costs, the greater the degree of operating leverage.

Opportunity cost. The benefit lost when choosing one option precludes the benefits from an alternative option.

Paid-in capital. Sum of the balances in capital stock and capital in excess of par value accounts.

Payback period. Amount of time required for the cash inflows from a project to equal the cash outflows.

Predetermined overhead rate. An estimated rate used to apply factory overhead cost to a cost object.

Prepaid expense. An expenditure for future services that will be treated as expenses when the service is received (prepaid rent, prepaid insurance, etc.).

Present value. Value today of a future cash flow, discounted at some interest or discount rate.

Price/earnings ratio. The market value of a share of a corporation's common stock divided by the earnings per common share for the past year.

Qualified report (opinion). Auditor's report stating that the auditor was not able to satisfactorily examine all items considered relevant or that the auditor has doubts about some material item(s) reported in the financial statements.

Quality. The characteristics of a product or service as they relate to customer satisfaction.

Quick assets. Cash plus marketable securities and current receivables.

Quick ratio. Also known as the acid test ratio. Quick assets divided by current liabilities.

Relevant cost. A future cost that varies among alternatives.

Relevant range. Activity level over which variable costs are linear and for which fixed costs remain fixed.

Required rate of return. Cost of capital.

Residual income. The amount by which the income of a project or subunit of a firm exceeds the firm's cost of capital multiplied by the amount of capital invested in the project or subunit of the firm.

Retained earnings. Net income over the life of a corporation less all dividends.

Retained earnings statement. A statement which reconciles the beginning and the ending balances in the retained earnings account.

Revenue. The inflow of cash, increases in other assets or settlement of liabilities resulting from the sale of goods and services that constitute an organization's principal operations.

SEC (Securities and Exchange Commission). The agency which, among other duties, oversees the financial reporting practices of public corporations. The SEC usually allows the FASB to set accounting principles.

Semifixed costs. Costs that increase with activity in a stair-step fashion.

Semivariable costs. Costs that vary with activity but which are positive at zero activity level. Utility and cell phone bills with limited minutes of calls are examples of semivariable costs.

Sensitivity analysis. Also known as "what-if" analysis. Analyzes how changes in assumptions affect the outcome in cost-volume-profit studies.

Stakeholder. Anyone with a genuine interest in an organization's activities and outcomes.

Standard cost. A predetermined or budgeted cost of a unit of output.

Statement of cash flows. A schedule of cash receipts and payments for a given period of time. It classifies sources and uses of cash from operating, investing and financing activities.

Static budget. Fixed budget. Budget based on the level of output planned for the budget period.

Stock dividend. A dividend in which the firm distributes additional shares of capital stock instead of cash. The result is that shareholders now own more shares of a company's stock, but not a larger percentage of total stock.

Straight-line depreciation. Method in which periodic depreciation charges are all equal.

Sunk cost. A cost incurred in the past which except for possible income tax effects is irrelevant to current decisions.

10-K. The annual report which the SEC requires of publicly held corporations.

Total assets turnover. Sales divided by average total assets.

Total quality management. The continuous, ongoing effort to ensure high-quality products and understand and meet customer expectations.

Treasury shares. Capital stock issued and then purchased back by a corporation. Treasury shares reduce shareholders' equity.

Uncollectible account. An account receivable that an organization will not be able to collect.

Underapplied overhead. The amount by which actual overhead incurred exceeds the overhead applied to a product or service.

Unexpired cost. An asset.

Usage variance. Efficiency variance.

Valuation account. A contra account or adjunct account.

Value chain. An analytic tool firms use to identify the specific steps required to provide a product or service. These steps typically include research and development, design, production, marketing, distribution and customer service.

Variable costs. Costs that change with changes in the quantity of the cost driver.

Variance. Difference between budgeted and actual expenditures.

Volume variance. Production volume variance; less often, used to mean sales volume variance.

Window dressing. The attempt to make operating results or financial position more favorable than they would otherwise be.

Working capital. Current assets minus current liabilities.

Write off. To charge an asset to expense or loss; that is, to debit expense (or loss) and credit the asset.

APPENDIX C

ANSWERS TO END-OF-CHAPTER EXERCISES

1 The Basics

1 The type of account (asset, liability, owners' equity, revenue, expense) and the financial statements on which it belongs are as follows:

Account	Type	Financial Statement
Cash	asset	balance sheet
Depreciation expense	expense	income statement
Accumulated depreciation	contra asset	balance sheet
Accounts receivable	asset	balance sheet
Accounts payable	liability	balance sheet
Dividends	owners' equity	balance sheet
Prepaid rent	asset	balance sheet
Utilities expense	expense	income statement
Inventory	asset	balance sheet (also appears on the income statement as part of the cost of goods sold section)
Employee wages	expense	income statement
Income tax	expense	income statement
Interest payable	liability	balance sheet

2 The missing amounts for each firm are:

Table AppC.1

	Firm X	Firm Y	Firm Z
Total assets 12/31/11	$500,000	**$800,000**	$350,000
Total liabilities 12/31/11	200,000	450,000	**175,000**
Paid-in capital 12/31/11	30,000	100,000	50,000
Retained earnings 12/31/11	**270,000**	**250,000**	125,000
Net income for 2011	80,000	120,000	150,000
Dividends paid in 2011	30,000	50,000	**115,000**
Retained earnings 12/31/10	**220,000**	180,000	90,000

3   The income statement for 20X9 and the balance sheet for Proctor Company as of December 31, 20X9 are as follows:

Proctor Company
Income Statement for the Year Ended December 31, 20X9

Sales	$250,000
Less Cost of Goods Sold	130,000
Gross Profit	120,000
Less Selling and Administrative Expenses	42,000
Operating Income	78,000
Less Other Expenses – Interest	5,000
Earnings before Taxes	73,000
Less Income Tax Expense	12,000
Net Income	$61,000

Proctor Company
Balance Sheet as of December 31, 20X9

Assets		Liabilities and Owners' Equity	
Cash	$ 70,000	Accounts Payable	$20,000
Accounts Receivable	12,000	Long-Term Debt	40,000
Inventory	42,000	Total Liabilities	60,000
Equipment	$130,000	Common Stock	100,000
Less Accum. Dprn.	40,000	Retained Earnings*	54,000
Net Equipment	90,000		
Total Assets	$214,000	Total Liab. and O.E.	$214,000

* Retained Earnings 1/1/X9	$21,000
Plus Net Income	61,000
Less Dividends	(28,000)
Retained Earnings 12/31/X9	$54,000

Figure AppC.1

2 Costs, Cost Behavior and Cost Analysis

1 Opportunity costs are the benefits of forgone alternatives. Clearly, Adam's opportunity cost of starting his own restaurant includes his previous salary of $35,000 plus any forgone benefits. There may also be non-quantitative costs such as a sense of security knowing he had a steady paycheck coming in every month.

The opportunity cost of not leaving his job would have been the forgone profit from his own restaurant, which could be considerably more or less than $35,000. He would also forgo the satisfaction of being his own boss.

2 We can define cost as the amount of assets given up or the liability incurred in order to acquire some good or service. Assets are unexpired costs. Expenses are costs that have expired. As time passes, most assets expire and their costs become expenses. A machine's cost becomes depreciation expense. Prepaid rent becomes rent expense. The cost of inventory becomes the cost of goods sold upon its sale.

3 A **sunk cost** is a cost which has already been incurred and is irrelevant for decision making. A **variable cost** is a cost which changes in proportion to a cost driver. Costs often vary with changes in output, the number of batches produced and the number and complexity of an organization's products. A **product cost** is a cost attached to a product. It is matched against revenue when the product is sold. Direct material, direct labor and manufacturing overhead are examples of product costs. A **period cost** is a cost attached to a period of time. It is matched against revenue when it is incurred. General and administrative expenses are examples of period costs.

3 Cost-Volume-Profit Analysis

1 (a) The breakeven quantity for option one is $3,000 ÷ ($1,000 − $700) = 10 bicycles. The breakeven quantity for option two is zero. For option two, she has no fixed costs. If she sells no bicycles, she will have merely broken even at the show.
(b) To solve this problem, determine the profit equation for each

option and set them equal to each other as follows and solve for X.
X equals units sold.

Option 1   ($1,000 − $700)X − $3000 = ($1,000 − $100 −
$700)X   Option 2
$300X − $3,000 = $200X
$100X = $3,000
X = 30

Olivia will be indifferent at the level of 30 units. Each option will
provide a profit of $6,000 at that level of sales.
(c)   If sales exceed 30 units, Olivia will prefer option 1.

2   (a) Denali must sell 247 skateboards to break even.
$19,000 (total fixed costs) ÷ $77 (contribution margin per unit) =
246.76
(b) Denali must sell 606 skateboards to earn an after-tax profit of
$18,000.
[$19,000 + (18,000 ÷ 0.65)] ÷ $77 = 606

3   (a) Their contribution margin per dinner is $30 − $18 = $12.
(b) Their breakeven quantity per month is $5,000 ÷ $12 = 417.
(c) Their after-tax profit last month was [(500 × $12) − $5,000] × (1
− 0.20) = $800.
(d) Their anticipated after-tax profit for next month is
[(600 × $12 − $5,000] × (1 − 0.20) = $1,760.
(e) In order to earn an after-tax profit of $2,000 per month they need
to sell
[$5,000 + ($2,000 ÷ 0.80)] ÷ $12 = 625 meals.

4   Ten percent increase:

	Ye Olde Furniture	Ye Newe Furniture
Sales	$1,100,000	$1,100,000
Variable costs	770,000	550,000
Contribution margin	330,000	550,000
Fixed costs	200,000	400,000
Operating income	$130,000	$150,000

Ten percent decrease:

	Ye Olde Furniture	Ye Newe Furniture
Sales	$900,000	$900,000
Variable costs	630,000	450,000
Contribution margin	270,000	450,000
Fixed costs	200,000	400,000
Operating income	$70,000	$50,000

Ye Newe Furniture has a greater degree of operating leverage (more fixed costs as compared to variable costs) than Ye Olde Furniture. Consequently, similar changes in volume will have a greater impact on profits.

4   Decision Making I: The Basics

1   (a) **Relevant information** is expected future data that varies among alternatives. If you include any data in your decision model that does not fit that description and if that information has an impact on your decision, you will arrive at a less than optimal outcome.

(b) **Incremental analysis** is the examination of expected revenues, costs, cash flows, profits, etc. from following one course of action versus another.

(c) A **sunk cost** is a cost which has already been incurred and is irrelevant for decision making.

(d) An **opportunity cost** represents the income or contribution margin lost from forgone opportunities.

(e) **Allocation** is the systematic assignment of joint costs to cost objects. For example, a retail store might allocate the cost of the controller's office to each of the different sales departments.

(f) **Differential costs** are sometimes referred to as incremental or marginal costs. They are costs which differ from one decision to another.

2   Qualitative advantages of making rather than buying a component could include ensuring the quality of the component, ensuring the availability of the component and keeping the labor force fully employed.

3 (a)

	90%	70%
Material	$14.00	$14.00
Labor	6.00	6.00
Variable overhead	5.00	5.00
Total variable costs	$25.00	$25.00
Fixed overhead	5.00	6.43
Total cost	$30.00	$31.43

(b) Yes, DBL, Inc. should accept the offer. The offer ($28.00) is greater than the variable costs ($25.00) per unit that would be incurred if the order was accepted.

(c) The firm's total contribution margin would be increased by $30,000 and total fixed costs would not be affected. Hence, the overall impact on DBL, Inc.'s profits would be $30,000.

(d) The lowest amount DBL, Inc. should accept is $25.00 per order. Anything less than that would result in a loss.

(e) By accepting the offer they would be able to keep their labor force fully employed and perhaps be able to open a new market for their products.

4

	Accept Offer	Do Not Accept	Difference
Revenue	$1,300	$1,344	$44.00
Attendant salary	56	112	56.00
Contribution margin	$1,244	$1,232	$12.00

This is pretty much a toss-up. The $12.00 difference is insignificant. Other factors to consider are: What impact will this decision have on regular customers? Will he lose some? Can Joe develop an ongoing relationship with the out-of-town hockey teams?

5 Decision Making II: Capital Budgeting Decisions

1 A dollar received today has a greater value today than a dollar to be received a year from now. A dollar to be received a year from now

has a greater value today than a dollar to be received two years from now, and so on. The reasons for this are threefold:

- Inflation erodes the purchasing power of a dollar.
- The longer the time before a dollar is to be received, the greater the risk it will not be.
- If a dollar is received today it can be invested and earn interest.

2   Depreciation, itself, has no impact on cash flow. It is a non-cash expense which reduces taxable income, thereby reducing a firm's tax expense. The result is lower taxes, which is equivalent to cash inflow.

3   According to the present value of the annuity table (Table B) in the appendix to Chapter 5, the interest factor of an annuity for five years at 12 percent is 3.605. The present value of the annuity is $500 × 3.605 = **$1,802.50**.

4   $500 × 0.567 = $283.50. One way to think of this is: if you put $283.50 in the bank today at 12 percent interest, compounded annually, at the end of five years the principal and interest earned would equal $500.00.

5   Since Kathy Smith's savings are constant, they represent an annuity for five years. The present value of her savings is 3.993 × $30,000 = $119,790. The net present value of this project, therefore, is $119,790 − $100,000 = $19,790.

6   The IRR is that rate of return which equates the present value of cash outflows with the present value of cash inflows. In this case it is $100,000 ÷ $30,000 = 3.333. Going to the chart we find that 3.333 lies between 15 and 16 percent. Using Excel we find that it is precisely 15.2 percent.

7   The subjective factors she might want to consider depend on the particular circumstances at hand. Possible factors include the impact

the purchase might have on her employees, other stakeholders and the environment. The impact the purchase might have on her firm's image in the marketplace could also be a factor.

8 (a) The annual cash flow from this investment is calculated as follows:

Annual revenues	$70,000
Cash expenses	30,000
Depreciation	20,000
Taxable income	20,000
Tax (30%)	6,000
Operating income	14,000
Depreciation	20,000
Annual cash flow	$34,000

(b) The NPV is calculated as:

Cash outflow for purchase, period 0	$(80,000) × 1	= $(80,000)
Annual cash inflow, periods 1–4	$ 34,000 × 3.170 =	107,780
Net present value		$27,780

(c) The discounted payback period is approximately 2.82 years.

Year 1 $34,000 × 0.909	= $30,906
Year 2 34,000 × 0.826	= 28,084
Year 3 34,000 × 0.751 × 0.82 =	20,938
Total	$79,928

(d) The project's ARR is $14,000 ÷ $40,000 = 35%.
(e) Yes, Bijou, Inc. should undertake this investment. It provides a positive NPV of $27,780 when its cash flows are discounted at the firm's cost of capital.

6 Planning and Budgeting

1 Budgets communicate an organization's goals and set forth expectations in financial terms. They help answer such questions as:

- What level of sales will we need this year to achieve our desired rate of return?
- What are our budgeted costs?
- Which costs are fixed and which are variable?

The budget can also provide an estimate of the resources and funding a firm will need to achieve its operating goals.

2 To ensure that you have adequate, but not excessive, cash available when it is needed.

3 1 (g) 2 (f) 3 (e) 4 (b) 5 (d) 6 (c) 7 (a)

4

Beans	Qtr. 1	Qtr. 2	Qtr. 3	Qtr. 4
Need for production (lb)	25,000	22,500	27,500	22,000
Need for ending inventory	11,250	13,750	11,000	13,500
Total needed	36,250	36,250	38,500	35,500
Less beginning inventory	12,500	11,250	13,750	11,000
Need to purchase (lb)	23,750	25,000	24,750	24,500
Purchase price	$47,500	$50,000	$49,500	$49,000

Rice				
Need for production (lb)	50,000	45,000	55,000	44,000
Need for ending inventory	22,500	27,500	22,000	27,000
Total needed	72,500	72,500	77,000	71,000
Less beginning inventory	25,000	22,500	27,500	22,000
Need to purchase (lb)	47,500	50,000	49,500	49,000
Purchase price	$142,500	$150,000	$148,500	$147,000

5

Table Appendix C.2

	January	February	March	Total
Beginning cash balance	$20	20	25	$20
Collections	50	60	60	170
Total cash available	70	80	85	190
Less disbursements:				
Purchases	30	35	50	115
Operating expenses	20	20	30	70
Total disbursements	50	55	80	185
Cash balance	20	25	5	5
Balance vs. minimum ($15)	5	10	(10)	(10)
Borrowed			10	10
Repaid				
Ending cash balance	$20	25	15	$15

7   Control

1   Static budget analysis merely shows the difference between budgeted revenues and costs at budgeted volume and actual revenues and
costs at actual volume. If there is (as there usually is) a difference
between actual and budgeted volumes, the difference between actual
revenues and costs and budgeted revenues and costs could be due
to volume, price or usage or some combination thereof. The static
budget does not reveal the cause of the differences; it only shows
that there is a difference. Flexible budget analysis disaggregates these
variances to show their causes.

2   The use of standard costs permits management by exception.
Management can thereby concentrate on those areas that are not
going according to plan. By using a system of standard costs and analyzing the variances between actual and standard costs, management
is in a position to concentrate on those areas where improvement is
needed.

3   Keep in mind that variances don't tell us what is wrong, but
where to look. Furthermore, functions within an organization are

usually interactive. That is, actions taken by the purchasing department often have an impact on production departments. The purchasing department could get a "real deal" on inventory that turns out to be sub-par, which in turn requires additional processing labor, thus creating an unfavorable labor efficiency variance.

4 (a, b and c)

	Actual	Variance	Flexible Budget	Volume Variance	Static Budget
Units	10,500		10,500		10,000
Sales	$2,050,000	$50,000(U)	$2,100,000	$100,000(F)	$2,000,000
Direct material	339,063	24,063(U)	315,000	15,000(U)	300,000
Direct labor	625,000	5,000(F)	630,000	30,000(U)	600,000
Var. overhead	620,000	10,000(F)	630,000	30,000(U)	600,000
Contrib. margin	$465,937	$59,063(U)	$525,000	$25,000(F)	$500,000
Fixed overhead	125,000	25,000(U)	100,000	–0–	100,000
Fixed S&A	240,000	10,000(F)	250,000	–0–	250,000
Net income	100,937	$74,063(U)	$175,000	$25,000(F)	$150,000

(d) Answers to this question can vary a great deal. The unfavorable material price variance might have occurred because the firm purchased a higher grade of material than standards called for. The superior quality of the material, in turn, could have given rise to a favorable efficiency variable. Likewise, the unfavorable wage rate variance could be due to a new incentive plan which paid off in greater efficiency. Answers such as this are, of course, pure speculation, and only after investigation would we know what actually gave rise to the variances.

Kruger and Huff Enterprises
Analysis of Flexible Budget Variances

Direct Material Variances

	Purchased			Used	
Actual	Price Variance	Std. Price × Act. Quant.	Std. Price × Act. Quant.	Usage Variance	Flexible Budget
32,000 ft		32,000 ft	31,000 ft		10,500 units × 3 ft
× $10,596		× $10	× $10		× $10
$339,063	$19,063(U)	$320,000	$310,000	$5,000(F)	$315,000

Direct Labor Variances

	Actual	Wage Rate Variance	Std. Price × Act. Quant.	Efficiency Variance	Flexible Budget
	41,500 hrs		41,500hrs		10,500 × 4
	× $15.06		× $15.00		× $15.00
	$625,000	$2,500(U)	$622,500	$7,500(F)	$630,000

Variable Overhead Variances

Actual Var. O'head	Spending Variance	Actual Input Quantity × Rate		Efficiency Variance	Flexible Budget
		$625,000			$630,000
		× $1/labor			× $1/labor $
$620,000	$4,500(U)	$625,000		$5,000(F)	$630,000

Figure AppC.2

8   Allocation

1

Table AppC.3

Solution: Traditional

	Dinner Baskets		Dessert Packages	
Direct materials	($36,000 ÷ 6,000)	$6.00	($8,000 ÷ 2,000)	$4.00
Direct labor	($18.00 ÷ 4)	4.50	($18.00 ÷ 2)	9.00
Overhead	[($43,000 ÷ 2,500) ÷ 4]	4.30	[($43,000 ÷ 2,500) ÷ 2]	8.60
Total cost per unit		$14.80		$21.60

Table AppC.4

Solution: ABC

		Dinner Baskets		Dessert Packages
Direct materials		$6.00		$4.00
Direct labor		4.50		9.00
Overhead:				
Material handling	(6,000 units × $2) ÷ 6,000 baskets	2.00	(2,000 units × $2) ÷ 2,000 packages	2.00
Dehydrating	(4,000 hours × $2) ÷ 6,000 baskets	1.33	(2,000 hours × $2) ÷ 2,000 packages	2.00
Assembly	(3,000 inspections × $0.50) ÷ 6,000 baskets	0.25	(3,000 inspections × $0.50) ÷ 2,000 packages	0.75
Tests	(4,000 × $2.00) ÷ 6,000 baskets	1.33	(2,000 × $2.00) ÷ 2,000 packages	2.00
Total overhead per unit		$4.91	Total overhead per unit	$6.75
Total cost per unit		$15.41	Total cost per unit	$19.75

Now that we've crunched the numbers, consider the solution and its implications for management by considering the remaining questions in Chapter 8.

2 The traditional or so-called "peanut butter" approach to allocating overhead costs spreads them across the different products using a single overhead application rate that treats all overhead costs as if they all increase and decrease proportionately with production volume. Consequently, some products will be over-costed and some under-costed. Also, this method of allocation offers no insight into what causes overhead costs and thus gives management no information for controlling them.

3 If products' costs are not reasonably accurate, managers cannot make proper pricing, marketing or production decisions. Sales will be lost if we base sales prices on costs that we think are higher than they actually are, and contribution margins will be lost if we base

prices on costs that were actually more than what our accounting records indicated.

4   They can use ABC costing to make decisions regarding cost control, pricing, product mix and organizing production.

5   Signs that might indicate that House of the Sun Foods is not providing its management with the information they need are: (i) Does the accounting system reflect the fact that some products are more difficult to produce than others? (ii) Are the profit margins on some of the products hard to explain? (iii) Has the production technology changed? (iv) Has there been a change in the product mix?

9   Financial Statement Analysis

1   The degree to which a firm can finance its current, ongoing operations. Low liquidity ratios indicate a firm might find it difficult or even be unable to pay its suppliers, meet payroll and service its short-term debt.

2   Current assets ÷ current liabilities = current ratio. In 2009, the current ratio was $921,712 ÷ $179,287 = **5.14:1**. In 2008 the current ratio was $872,519 ÷ $173,189 = **5.04:1**. This would indicate that the firm was slightly more liquid in 2009.

3   Quick assets ÷ current liabilities = quick ratio. For 2009 the quick ratio was ($386,664 + $22,759 + $226,548) ÷ $179,287 = **3.55:1**. For 2008 the quick ratio was ($230,617 + $22,433 + $299,585) ÷ $173,189 = **3.19:1**. Yes, our findings in exercise 2 are confirmed.

4   Leverage ratios reveal the percentage of assets financed by debt and/or financed by equity. They measure a firm's solvency.

5   Debt ÷ equity. $215,655 ÷ $997,228 = **0.22:1**

6   Debt ÷ total assets. $215,655 ÷ $1,212,883 = **17.8:1**

7   Times interest earned = earnings before interest and taxes ÷ interest expense. For 2009, C.S.'s times interest earned was $89,850 ÷ $22,829 = **3.94**. For 2008, it was $126,243 ÷ $31,196 = **4.05**.

8   The difference in the figures for 2008 and 2009 is small and insignificant. Based on the times interest earned calculation, the banker would be just as likely to loan money to C.S. in 2009 as in 2008.

9   Activity ratios reveal how actively a firm uses its various assets. They are based on the notion that there is some best level of assets for any given firm at any given time. A low ratio possibly indicates the company has invested too much in an asset. A high ratio possibly indicates the firm could need to acquire more of the asset.

10   The inventory turnover is cost of sales ÷ inventory. For 2009, C.S.'s inventory turnover was $719,945 ÷ $222,161 = **3.24** times. The number of days' sales in inventory is inventory ÷ average daily cost of goods sold. As of December 31, 2009 the number of days' sales in their inventory was $222,161 ÷ 1,972 = **112.7 days**.

11   Accounts receivable turnover = sales ÷ accounts receivable. For 2009 the accounts receivable turnover was $ 1,244,023 ÷ $226,548 = **5.49 times**. For 2008, it was $1,317,835 ÷ $299,585 = **4.4 times**.

12   It was considerably higher in 2009.

13   Accounts payable turnover = cost of goods sold ÷ accounts payable. For 2009, $719,945 ÷ $102,494 = **7.02 times**. For 2008, $750,024 ÷ $104,354 = **7.19 times**. This suggests that they did not pay their suppliers quite as fast in 2009 as they did in 2008, but the difference is rather slight.

14   Profitability ratios relate some measure of a firm's profit to some factor (e.g. sales, assets or owners' equity) involved in the earning process.

15   DuPont method: profit margin × turnover = return on assets

$$\underline{Net\ Income \div Sales} \quad \times \quad \underline{Sales \div Assets} \qquad = ROA$$

2009: $67,021 ÷ $1,244,023 × $1,244,023 ÷ $1,212,883 =
                    0.054 ×   1.026   **= 0.055**

2008: $95,047 ÷ $1,317,835 × S1,317,835 ÷ $1,148,236 =
                    0.072 ×   1.148   **= 0.083**

2008 was a better year for C.S. They not only had a higher profit margin, but they also had a higher asset turnover. Consequently, their return on assets was considerably higher in 2008 as compared with 2009.

16   Return on equity ≠ net income ÷ owners' equity. $67,021 ÷ $997,228 = **0.067**. 2009 was not a particularly good year for C.S. Nevertheless, they were still able to earn a return on equity of 6.7 percent (0.067). Their return on assets for the year (0.055) was less than their return on equity. This indicates that they used debt wisely.

INDEX